He's Coming Soon!

JAMES HORVATH

CREATION HOUSE
BOOKS ABOUT SPIRIT-LED LIVING
ORLANDO, FLORIDA

Copyright © 1995 by James Horvath
All rights reserved
Printed in the United States of America
Library of Congress Catalog Card Number: 95-69247
International Standard Book Number: 0-88419-395-0

Creation House
Strang Communications Company
600 Rinehart Road
Lake Mary, FL 32746
Fax: (407) 333-7100

Acknowledgments

Glory to the triune God: the Father, Son and the Holy Spirit.

To my wife, Michele, and our children, Jonathan, Rachael and Joseph, for their positive encouragement.

To my mentors, Robert Crabtree and Richard Exley, who discipled me.

To David Shibley who guided me through the writing process.

To the charismatic ministers whose writings have influenced my life and ministry.

To my instructors at Central Bible College and Oral Roberts University who have had a part in shaping my theological thinking.

To my staff and congregation at Calvary Lighthouse Church who have worked on this project.

To Steve Strang, John Mason, Deborah Poulalion and the staff of Creation House for their diligence in editing and promoting this book.

Contents

Introduction

Perhaps the most evangelistic doctrine of the charismatic movement is eschatology, or the study of end times. My own conversion was a result of a series of evangelistic campaigns focused on the end times. Today the saved and the unsaved alike are talking about the signs of the times, the Antichrist, 666 and the battle of all battles, Armageddon.

While traditional theology has debated whether the rapture will take place at the beginning, middle or end of the tribulation, charismatic theology has focused end-time teaching on world evangelization. For the typical charismatic believer, eschatology is a tool to use daily to win souls. When charismatics speak of the rapture or the great White Throne judgment, it is normally in the context of an altar call or some other soul-winning event. Because of this, I have written an entire chapter on the charismatic thrust toward world evangelization by the year 2000.

Charismatics are surprisingly united in their doctrine. While writing this volume on charismatic theology, I was often asked, "How are you going to establish common ground among such a diverse group of people?" I have found that although charismatics are diversified in style of ministry, they are unified in the area of theology.

For example, most charismatic pastors and teachers take the Word of God literally, believing in a literal rapture, a literal second coming, a literal millennium, a literal judgment, a literal heaven and hell, and a literal new heaven and new earth. The majority are premillennialists (meaning that Jesus will return before the millennium), and most are pretribulationists.

Another strength I found while reviewing the writings of these men and women of God was their ability to remain optimistic in the face of trouble. They do not believe in running to the mountains with their canned goods to hide. Rather, they believe in standing in the last days, possessing the land and winning the world for Christ. Though they know the Word of God says that tribulation is ahead, charismatics believe that they will be spared from God's wrath in the tribulation (1 Thess. 5:9).

During my graduate studies at Oral Roberts University, I was able to sit under many of the leading charismatic teachers: David Yonggi Cho, Benny Hinn, Lester Sumrall, Kenneth Copeland, Bob Yandian, Oral Roberts, Richard Roberts, Casey Treat, T. L. Osborn, Roberts Liardon, Freda Lindsay, Reinhard Bonnke, Marilyn Hickey, Charles Blake,

Billy Joe Daugherty, Tommy Reid, Karl Strader, John Hagee, John Avanzini, Jack Hayford, Charles Capps, Hilton Sutton, Jerry Savelle, Stephen Strang, Fred Price, Richard Exley, Norvel Hayes — and this list could be expanded. Regarding the basic systems of theology, I found them to be in agreement.

One course that I found especially helpful, "Signs and Wonders," was designed by Dr. Paul Chappell. The idea for this class came from a course that Fuller Theological Seminary had attempted with John Wimber. Dr. Chappell had the resources and the people to expand the idea. Eventually, people even informally called the ORU seminary the "signs and wonders seminary." Dr. Larry Lea became the dean of the seminary. He and Dr. Chappell were able to bring the greatest charismatic ministries together to teach us charismatic theology.

I was honored to be a member of the pilot course, and I participated in it for the next three years. My conclusion from my studies is that charismatic theology is strong because it is practical.

Systematic theology was never meant to be difficult to understand. In this volume, I have taken the most evangelistic doctrine of the church — the doctrine of end times — and tried to portray accurately the charismatic interpretation of it. What we believe about the coming of Jesus should motivate us to live right and win the world around us to Christ. May you find the doctrine of the end times easy to understand, and may this book help you apply it in your life.

1

THE TIME IS CRITICAL

Widespread Interest in Signs of the Times

Do you remember the first time you had an experience with the Word of God that caused you to stop and say, "God really does speak through the Bible!"? I do. I had just returned from a vacation in Florida where I stayed with a family who gave me a *Good News for Modern Man* New Testament. I was twenty-two years old, unsaved and unchurched, and I thought I had no need for a Bible. I discarded it into a box.

Now, I must back up and tell you why this Christian family had given me the Bible. While I was in their home, I brought up the subject of the end times and how close the end of the world was. I told them about earthquakes, famines, nuclear weapons, Russia and the Antichrist.

The wife was amazed, but not about my knowledge of the end times. She was amazed that I knew all of this — and yet was not saved. I didn't even know what *saved* meant. You see, the circle of people I was running around with talked about the end of the world in light of what they heard in the daily media. At work or at a party, the topic seemed to surface regularly.

Some time after I returned from Florida, I was having a conversation with a friend. I was telling him the Bible said that the kings of the East would invade from the east in the battle of Armageddon. He challenged me: "Horvath, you keep saying all of this stuff is in the Bible. Show me."

I had not been in a church since I was fourteen years old. My family had attended a mainline denominational church where no one carried a Bible. I didn't know Genesis from Revelation. How was I going to find this in the Bible?

Unless you've had a similar experience, you probably won't believe me. I located that *Good News* New Testament I had thrown in the box, opened it somewhere in the book of Revelation, stuck my finger in and started reading out loud to my friend. To his — and my — surprise, I found the exact scriptures I had told him were there (16:12), and I wasn't even saved yet!

It was shortly after this experience that I, and many of my friends who often discussed the end times, got saved. This is why I believe teaching about the end of the world is extremely important. Not only were we drawn to salvation through this doctrine, but we were discipled in end-time teaching as well. We read everything we could about it and shared with all those around us. We even wrote letters to our families about how they could be saved if they missed the rapture. At conversion, we were end-time fanatics.

I believe that many people who are not saved find the discussion of the end of the age enthralling. You and I are called by God to have our speech filled with grace and seasoned with salt to win this world to Christ (Col. 4:6). We are to be wise as serpents and harmless as doves as we fish for men (Matt. 10:16). I've found that people love to talk about the future. As you read this book, keep in mind that those people are all around you. God is preparing their hearts with questions even now. Study to show yourself approved as a good workman in this area (2 Tim. 2:15). God is just waiting to use you.

Daniel Foretold It

Why is there so much emphasis on the end-time doctrine in our day? I believe it is because Jesus is preparing the church for His soon-coming return. Jesus will return for a church that is without spot or wrinkle or any such thing (Eph. 5:27). In order for the church to become the "bride adorned" (Rev. 21:2,9), the body of Christ must first learn to walk in the revelation that it already has.

Daniel prophesied that the church would be prepared at Christ's return. An angel told Daniel to shut up the things which were revealed to him about the end times because these truths would not be known until the last days when many would be purified and made spotless (Dan. 12:9-10). There is an undercurrent flowing in the body of Christ today calling believers to holiness and purity in these last days.

I believe we have begun to see the unlocking of the end-time truths that Daniel envisioned. Charismatic theology is an imperative study in our hour because it thoroughly embraces the doctrine of the second coming. In the same way that Daniel pressed into visions and dreams, charismatics have pressed into the doctrine of the second coming of Christ. In almost every charismatic book or sermon series, the doctrine of end times is addressed.

Our consuming desire to understand the signs of the time and the end of the age has not caused us to run to the mountains and retreat. Actually, it has done just the opposite by leading us to win this world for Christ and to live holy lives, realizing that Jesus could return at any moment.

The theologians of the charismatic movement, such as Oral Roberts, Benny Hinn and Lester Sumrall, have had their ministries forged in the fire of end-time revelations.

Some in the body of Christ who disagree with their teachings may question the fact that I call these men theologians. But in my estimation, these men, and those I will quote in this book, are theologians. After all, what does the word *theology* mean? It is a composite of two Greek words: *theos* meaning "God," and *logos* meaning "the study or science of something." Theology is simply the study of God, who He is and what He says. Therefore, the study of charismatic end-time theology is what charismatics have found God to be saying about the end times.

As you proceed through this book, my first volume on charismatic theology, I believe that the quotations and revelations of these men and women of God will stir you as they have stirred me. The hour and the day we are living in are critical. The generation we are living in has more revelation and anointing than any other generation. Jesus could return at any moment, even before you finish this book!

Practical Application

It is my premise that one of the greatest strengths of charismatic theology is that it is practical. It is a theology for the common man. Many of the charismatic books from which I will quote are the result of transcribed sermons. Sermons have a strong tendency to be practical. Therefore, I have chosen to include at the end of each chapter a nugget of practical application.

Our first nugget applies end-time theology to our daily lives. We should live every day as if Jesus could return at any moment, yet we should also plan to occupy until He comes. Ask yourself the question, If I knew that Jesus would return today, how would I spend my last hours on the earth? I do not believe you would run out and buy a steak dinner at a local restaurant. I believe you would run out to your neighbors, friends and relatives and tell them about Christ.

We need to maximize our daily schedules. Time is short, and it is our most precious commodity. What will we do today to further the kingdom of God?

Kenneth Copeland in his book *Honor — Walking in Honesty, Truth and Integrity,* says that in the last days we must stay spiritually nourished. "The closer we get to that day, the more we in the Church are going to have to learn more and more how to schedule our work time around the Word instead of trying to schedule the Word around our work time."[1]

Our theology should motivate us not only with our schedules but also with our priorities. We should do all we can to be a part of the great end-time plan of God to win this world for Christ.

2

THE IMMINENT
RETURN OF CHRIST

Common Doctrine Among Charismatics

Let me preface this discussion on the doctrine of eschatology, or end times, with my observation that most charismatics are extremely united on this topic. For example, most charismatics believe in a literal rapture of the church and a literal tribulation period. Most believe that Jesus could return at any moment for His church, but would be quick to agree that no man knows the day nor the hour of Christ's return (Matt. 24:36).

Charismatic theology is practical, so charismatics interpret their societies in light of Scripture. Jesus gave us a list of signs that would exist in the last generation. It is widely believed among charismatics that all of the necessary signs are fulfilled for Christ to return for the church. Theologically, this is called imminence.

Imminence, by definition, means that there is nothing which stands in the way of the return of Jesus for His church. Reinhard Bonnke in his book *Evangelism by Fire*, writes an entire chapter on "The Last Hour." Bonnke says, "The Bible's insistence that this is the last hour is a unique and special doctrine called imminence." He says that many in the church do not understand how near we are. "Many ease back into thinking there are still four months to harvest." Then Bonnke uses the apostle Paul to illustrate his point. "Paul lived as if the end of all things was at hand, as if the dropping of the final curtain was always imminent."[1]

C. P. Nelson, a pioneer in charismatic/Pentecostal theology, wrote an entire section in his book, *Bible Doctrines*, on the doctrine of the imminent return of Christ. He said that the rapture and the second coming of Christ are "the imminent and blessed hope of the church (1 Thess. 4:16-17; Rom. 8:23; Titus 2:13; 1 Cor. 15:51-52)."[2]

Dr. Roy Hicks says that this doctrine of imminence is so critical that if we as writers do not warn people of the lateness of the hour, we do them an "eternal, tragic disservice." Hicks emphasizes that "multitudes of sincere people have become caught up in the daily round of temporal activities." Dr. Hicks is correct in his challenge. It is the job of those who write theology, especially eschatology (end-time doctrine), to warn our audiences about the lateness of the hour.[3]

> And now, little children, abide in him; that, when he shall appear, we may have confidence, and not be ashamed before him at his coming (1 John 2:28).

R. A. Torrey speculated on John's instructions: "There

may be many reasons why we should abide in the Lord Jesus but the pre-eminent reason in John's mind was that Jesus was coming again and that if we were to have confidence and not be ashamed before Him when He did come, we must be abiding in Him."[4]

The majority of charismatics believe that Jesus will return in their lifetimes. Smith Wigglesworth, a Pentecostal fore-runner of the charismatic movement, believed that Jesus would return in his lifetime. W. Hacking, in his book *Smith Wigglesworth Remembered*, says "Brother Wigglesworth believed with all his heart that he would not die, but would live on to see the Rapture."[5]

Several years ago we had Dr. Richard Eby as a guest lecturer at our church. Dr. Eby, who was in his seventies then, said he had a vision in which he went to heaven. Jesus told him that He would return in Eby's lifetime.

Dr. Lester Sumrall, who is in his eighties, makes similar statements concerning the return of Christ in his lifetime. In the late 1980s, Dr. Lester Sumrall was one of the keynote speakers at the International Charismatic Bible Ministries conference held annually at Oral Roberts University. The focus of his lecture was the second coming of Christ. He stated emphatically that Jesus would return in or around the year 2000.

In his book *Time Bomb in the Middle East — Countdown to Armageddon*, Sumrall states that the countdown to judgment began about the year 1900, when the latter rain began (James 5:7). "I believe we are in the last of the last days, and living in the most exciting times of all history as we watch prophecy being fulfilled before our eyes and a great harvest of souls come into the Kingdom of God."[6]

Mario Murillo heralds the same idea in his work *Fresh Fire*. "Scripture teaches a unique balance in end time behavior." Murillo calls it being "*edge-wise*, living at the edge of time, fully realizing the imminent return of the

Lord, yet being wise to seize the opportunity to glorify God patiently, deliberately, and with excellence."[7]

The doctrine of imminence is critical to charismatics because it drives us to evangelism. No other doctrine equips and motivates the church like the doctrine of the end times. When we grasp the truth Scripture reveals, that Jesus could return at any moment, in the twinkling of an eye, then we are driven and compelled to win our world to Christ. This was the key to the early church's motivation and is one of the keys to charismatic success in world evangelization.

Practical Application

Early in my walk with Christ, I recall my pastor asking the congregation the question, "If Jesus came back tomorrow, what would you *not* want to be caught doing?" The practical side of the doctrine of imminence is that Jesus could return at any moment, and that fact should cause us to live holy lives. Not only should we not be caught doing what we shouldn't, but we should be caught doing what we should.

3

END-TIME HARVEST

A Day With God Is As a Thousand Years

Charismatics and Pentecostals are now, and have been for some time, looking for something to happen by the year 2000. One scripture is often used to support their view that Jesus will return on or around the year 2000.

> But, beloved, be not ignorant of this one thing, that one day is with the Lord as a thousand years, and a thousand years as one day (2 Pet. 3:8).

Charismatic teachers, including Lester Sumrall, Charles

Capps and Rod Parsley, teach that on or about the year 2000 mankind will have existed for six thousand years. They quote the biblical record that from Adam to Jesus was four thousand years, and from the birth of Jesus to the year 2000 will be two thousand years.

Take this thought in conjunction with God's concept of the Sabbath being the seventh day, and a day with the Lord being a thousand years. Six days would equal six thousand years. Therefore, earth and all of God's created order are due for a sabbatical of a thousand years, and according to some charismatic theology, it is about to happen.

Gordon Lindsay, founder of Christ for the Nations Institute, and an outstanding Pentecostal/charismatic theologian, makes a reference to this concept in one of his books. He titled the chapter "Man's 6,000 Years Completed — 2000 A.D." Dr. Lindsay had a true burden to write and preserve theology, especially end-time theology. In his 1968 work, *The World: 2000 A.D.*, Lindsay says: "According to Bible chronology, there was from Adam's creation until Christ some 4,000 years. This means including the present dispensation approximately 5,968 years have elapsed since the fall of Adam — or nearly *six of God's days*." Lindsay concluded from all the facts he could access that Jesus would come before the year 2000. He writes, "All signs indicate that this time of trouble will occur before the year 2000."[1]

Another great charismatic figure over the years, Rex Humbard, writes the same thing. In Humbard's sermon "Will the United States Fight in World War III?" he states, "There were 2,000 years until the time of the flood, 2,000 years from the flood until the coming of Christ and the fulfillment of that prophecy; and now almost 2,000 years have passed since then."

Humbard then quotes Matt. 24:22, "And except those days should be shortened, there should no flesh be saved: but for the elect's sake those days shall be shortened."

Humbard believes this means that this is the last dispensation. He writes, "This Holy Ghost dispensation will not live out its 2,000 years. God will cut it short. The signs of the times are at hand."[2]

Lester Sumrall in his book *I Predict 2000 A.D.*, predicts that a whole host of signs will occur by the year 2000. He accurately predicted the fall of Russia, a move toward more international policing, and increasing foreign influence on the U.S. economy. Dr. Sumrall writes, "I predict the absolute fullness of man's operation on planet Earth by the year 2000 A.D. Then Jesus Christ shall reign from Jerusalem for 1,000 years."[3]

The emphasis on the year 2000 is not new. I personally believe it is from the heart of God, by His design. God's desire is for us to fulfill His Word to preach the gospel in all the world. The year 2000 is a major mile marker in human history and represents a target date for that goal.

World Evangelization by the Year 2000?

Is it the will of God to reach this world by the year 2000? Just ask Morris Cerullo that question! In his biography Morris Cerullo tells of an incredible vision God gave him to reach the world by the year 2000. At the 1989 Morris Cerullo World Conference, he announced, "God has given me a divine mandate to reach one billion souls for His glory before the year 2000." In this seven-step outline Cerullo shared his strategy to train and equip the national pastors of the world:

1. Spiritual unity

2. Bestowal of a new mantle on foreign nations

3. Training foreign nationals

4. Mass evangelistic crusades

5. Use of satellite linkups

6. Use of television and radio by nationals

7. Training in spiritual warfare[4]

A member of my congregation has been a longtime supporter of Morris Cerullo's ministry, and she recently gave me a large portion of her *Victory Miracle Library*, a monthly magazine designed to train God's Victorious Army. Morris wrote in this monthly magazine, "We recognize that the upcoming, phenomenal end-time waves of the Holy Spirit are imminent! We have our marching orders...we are preparing to reach one billion souls for Jesus before the year 2000!"[5]

The doctrine of imminence affects the way we charismatics view world evangelization — and the way we live. Charismatics are very serious about world evangelization. When we understand that nothing stands in the way of the return of Christ, our priorities are challenged to see how our world can be won to Christ.

Dr. David Shibley, founder of Global Advance, addresses charismatic evangelization in his book *A Force in the Earth*. I had dinner with Dr. Shibley recently, and he spoke of the vision he has to see the charismatic churches of the United States impact the nations of the world by training those nations' pastors. I believe with all my heart that Dr. Shibley has a call of God to funnel resources and talents from charismatic churches in the United States into the entire world.

When Dr. Shibley spoke to my church several years ago, he shared with me a most incredible truth. He sees the strength of the charismatic movement as spirit-led evangelization. Shibley has challenged the evangelical movement to look at the success of the charismatics.[6] One cannot ignore that almost every major city of the world has large, Pentecostal/charismatic churches.

William DeArteaga, in his book *Quenching the Spirit*, addresses the strength of the charismatic movement being empowered by the Holy Spirit to win the world to Christ. He says the church in the last 150 years has come into its own in terms of operating in the gifts of the Spirit as the New Testament church operated. DeArteaga primarily sees this taking place in Pentecostal and charismatic settings. He concludes, "Projections indicate that by the end of the century the majority of Christians will belong to churches that accept and practice the gifts of the Holy Spirit as normal in Christian life."[7]

I believe that one of the reasons for the success of the charismatic movement is the empowerment by the Holy Spirit in light of the biblical doctrine of the second coming of Christ. As we view our world from the possibility of Christ returning at any moment, we sense the lateness of the hour and the urgency for the anointing of the Holy Spirit that biblical writers experienced in their day (1 John 2:18-20; Joel 2:28; Is. 35:1-10; Acts 2:17,41).

In the last decade of this millennium, the Holy Spirit has begun a major thrust among charismatics as well as the entire body of Christ toward the whole world being evangelized by the year 2000. There can be no question about it, the end of this millennium is viewed by charismatic believers as the target date for total world evangelization.

A Warning to Stay on Track

Mario Murillo gives the charismatic movement a very serious word of warning about its call to reach the world for Christ. First, he identifies the error in the teaching trends of some charismatics. He says that we have moved away from our commission to a global witness. Second, he says, "The Lord is sternly warning us to seek Him or forfeit our right to lead the next attack." We need a baptism of "fresh fire" to be used on a global level.[8] Mario Murillo is calling us to evangelism based on the truth that the return of the Lord is imminent.

In response to Mario Murillo's warning, we must also heed the warning of church history. In movements of God, men have often traditionalized what God was doing. When God moved in a new way to keep things fresh and on the edge, men often refused to follow, remaining boxed in by new and old traditions.

Charismatics must not institutionalize what God has done. God has used charismatics because His heart is after souls. Mario Murillo is saying that if we move away from this mandate, God will, as He historically has, find another group to use to win this world.

It is therefore imperative that we preach the message of the second coming and keep our people connected to God's heart for winning souls. God has designed into the Word a healthy tension to help the church stay focused on soul winning. That tension is that we are in the last days and Christ can return at any moment.

Much of our theology as charismatics was birthed from this cutting-edge tension from early Pentecostals like Smith Wigglesworth and John G. Lake. These men were so compelled by their end-time theology that they took their ministries around the world.

Women in End-Time Ministry

The theology of the early Pentecostal era was also responsible for the prolific development of women in ministry. One such woman was Maria Woodworth-Etter. Signs, wonders, healings and miracles were evident in Mrs. Woodworth-Etter's meetings, and as we might expect, she focused strongly on the doctrine of the second coming. Mrs. Woodworth-Etter had several visions of the second coming of Christ. One vision in particular was so strong that she said it was much of her motivation for ministry.[9]

Another woman God used mightily was Kathryn Kuhlman. I have spent numerous hours in the archives at Wheaton College researching the Kuhlman collection. She too drew regularly from her doctrine of eschatology.

Much of the collection at Wheaton College is comprised of Kathryn's television program, "I Believe in Miracles." On this program Kathryn interviewed people who had been healed in her meetings. She also interviewed key people who were impacting the body of Christ. One of my favorite interviews was with David du Plessis.

Du Plessis and Kuhlman agreed that they were living in the last days because of the great revival which was sweeping the earth. Du Plessis made reference to modern technology, saying the fact that Kathryn's program was even on television was the fulfillment of Christ's words that the gospel would be proclaimed all over the world. I wonder what they would say today if they could see how Christian television has expanded.

In another tape of Kathryn's, which profoundly impacted my own ministry, she shared the testimony of her father's death. At the funeral, as she was viewing the body, God spoke to her. "Kathryn, that is not your father in the casket. Your father is with Me." She said she then realized that "the body goes to the grave, but the spirit returns to be with the Lord."[10]

I have shared Kathryn's revelation at almost every funeral since then. Our doctrines of the second coming and life after death are the most practical doctrines of all. More people have been comforted by this area of theology than any other. Paul used end-time doctrine to comfort those in Thessalonica who had lost loved ones (1 Thess. 4:13-18). He concluded by saying, "Comfort one another with these words" (v. 18).

One of the clearest female charismatic voices calling women to ministry is Daisy Osborn. In her book *Five Choices*

26

for Women Who Win, Daisy spends the first eight chapters using eschatology to motivate women to be involved in ministry.

Daisy shares how she was motivated to ministry. She says that in many of our cultures women are taught to hold on to the accomplishments of their husbands to find their own identities. But one day Daisy was reading the Word of God when she received a revelation about judgment day. She was reading from Romans 14 in The Living Bible:

> Remember, each of us will stand personally before the Judgment Seat of God...Yes, each of us will give an account of himself to God (vv. 10,12).

Daisy realized that she would stand on her own before God on judgment day. Her husband, T. L. Osborn, is a great evangelist who has won hundreds of thousands to Christ. Yet he will stand on his own before God. Daisy understood for the first time that when God separates the sheep from the goats, it will be based on what they did and did not do (Matt. 25:31-46).

In a clarion call, Daisy challenges all women to be faithful servants of the talents that God has given to them. She says, "I had read these verses many times, but that day I discovered the seeds of truth that would have a profound and an eternal effect upon my life — and ultimately on the lives of women around the world."[11] Daisy calls women such as Gloria Copeland, Frances Hunter and Marilyn Hickey "winners" in this area.

When Fred Price was asked what he thought about women in ministry, he replied, "If God did not want women in ministry, He would not sanction their ministries by anointing them, and there would not be any results in them." He concludes, "The Bible says there is neither male nor female. We are all one in Christ Jesus."[12]

TBN and CBN: End-Time Tools

Another powerful arena of end-time harvest is media and communications. A Christian media forerunner, Trinity Broadcasting Network, has become a major charismatic tool. TBN is now one of the largest broadcasting networks in the world with 345 stations as of 1993. This includes fifty full-power stations, and the network is believing God for one hundred full-power stations before Jesus returns. Paul Crouch, in his book *I Had No Father But God*, says that when that happens, "I will be packing my bags for Glory! Surely that day is not too far away!"[13]

The growth of TBN is motivated by world evangelization and the doctrine of the imminent return of Jesus Christ. Paul and Jan Crouch can be heard on a regular basis saying, "We have a mandate to use the holy beamer and get the gospel into the nations of the world." When TBN launched their satellite, "Angel 1," Paul says that God gave them "His mighty *satellite angel* to reach our world with the Gospel of Christ."[14] God gave Paul and the TBN partners a prophetic promise from the Word:

> Ask of me, and I shall give thee the heathen for thine inheritance, and the uttermost parts of the earth for thy possession (Ps. 2:8).

TBN is also actively negotiating to build new stations in other nations. In the last chapter of Paul Crouch's book he explains how God unfolded His "master plan" for Christian TV for the whole world. "God's master plan is becoming gloriously apparent. TV stations at home and abroad, satellites, 'holy beamers,' shortwave radio, longwave radio, satellite dishes, cable stations, and now, *'They can all speak in other tongues!'* "[15]

TBN's vision is so great that they have built a translation center in Texas. You can often turn on TBN and see the people working to translate the programs into many languages. These programs are then dubbed over and broadcasted by satellite into the nations.

There are many other Christian-owned and operated stations throughout the world, including another incredible network, CBN. Christian Broadcasting Network has made great inroads into the secular arena. Pat Robertson and the Christian Broadcasting Network have successfully brought "The 700 Club" to the major secular networks. It reaches one million American households daily and airs in sixty countries of the world.[16]

The first paragraph of CBN's mission statement says, "The mission of CBN and its affiliated organizations is *to prepare* the United States of America, the nations of the Middle East, the Far East, South America and other selected nations of the world for the coming of Jesus Christ and the establishment of the Kingdom of God on the earth. Our ultimate goal is to achieve a time in history when 'the knowledge of the Lord will cover the earth as the waters cover the sea.'"[17]

Who can question the success of the Family Channel, a basic-cable television network? "The Family Channel now reaches approximately 95 percent of all cable households and 62 percent of all television households in the U.S. with its family-oriented entertainment programming."[18]

What a vision to cover the earth with the message of the gospel to prepare the earth for the return of Christ! I wonder what R. A. Torrey, one of the greatest soul-winning evangelists from the turn of the century, would say about the motivation of charismatics to preach in every nation before Jesus returns?

Torrey, who in his early ministry did not find much value in the doctrine of the second coming, wrote this as he matured, "To many the doctrine of the Second Coming of Christ seems like an impractical doctrine. I once so regarded it." Torrey continues, "But the day came when I found it was not only one of the most precious but also one of the most practical doctrines in the whole Bible." He concludes that this doctrine made him optimistic "even under the most discouraging circumstances."[19]

Practical Application

As a senior pastor of a growing church, I have identified the need to preach regularly on the second coming of Christ. I have done an eighteen-week, verse-by-verse series on the book of Revelation, complete with notes. Home Bible studies on the end times have a real attraction for the unsaved. People naturally have a God-given fascination with future events and the end of the world.

Last year I used one of Tommy Barnett's illustrated sermons, "What to Do If You Miss the Rapture." I gave a twelve-point message on how to survive during the tribulation. Each point was illustrated with a cast of more than fifty people. We are a sight-and-sound generation, and we must incorporate technology to be more effective in winning our world for Christ. In this sermon we used special effects to bring "war and rumors of wars" to life. Video projectors and subwoofers were used to create nuclear explosions. You could literally feel your pants shaking. The Antichrist and his armies came to life and marched into our sanctuary. People were even "raptured" from their chairs up to our ceiling with hoists and wires.

The last point of my message was, "Many who are saved during the tribulation will have to die a martyr's death." Then a real guillotine and an executioner came out and "beheaded" our key actor. I gave the altar call, and 120 people came running to the altars — and I mean running!

Charismatic theology is practical. It should motivate us to obey the command of Jesus to go "into all the world, and preach the gospel to every creature" (Mark 16:15). As we press on toward the year 2000, we should set both individual and corporate goals. All available technology should be used in creative ways to reach the world for Christ.

The year 2000 may or may not be the time of the return of Christ, but it gives us a date to aim toward. It has been said correctly that a man without a target will never know whether he hits or misses.

4

WHICH GENERATION WILL BE THE LAST?

Increasing Labor Pains

Several years ago the church I pastored had the opportunity to provide counselors at a concert Carman gave in our area. Carman Licciardello is a charismatic evangelist who uses contemporary Christian music to preach the gospel. We saw hundreds come to Christ at that concert.

In "We're Living in the Last Days," the last chapter of Carman's recent book, he cites Peter's sermon on the day of Pentecost. Peter quotes the prophet Joel, who says these are the "last days" (Acts 2:17). Using this text as proof,

32

Carman says, "The last days began when Jesus rose from the dead and the Holy Spirit was poured out on the Church."[1] Every generation of Christians has believed that their generation was the one in which Christ would return.

Is this the last generation? Mockers taunt that this has been believed for a long time (2 Pet. 3:3-4). Are they right, or did God in his great wisdom design a supernatural tension into the Word to keep every generation ready for the return of His Son?

The Tension of Generations Builds

The return of the Lord could be at any moment, yet no man knows the day or the hour. This expectation of His return without knowing when it will occur creates a healthy tension in Scripture — and in the believer. I believe God divinely placed this tension within Scripture to encourage us to live fruitful lives.

The apostle John believed that he was living in the last generation. He wrote in 1 John 2:18, "Little children, it is the last time; and as ye have heard that antichrist shall come, even now are there many antichrists; whereby we know that it is the last time."

John was the last apostle alive, and he knew about the brutal murders of the other apostles. According to accepted church tradition, James was killed by the sword of Herod, Peter was hung on a cross upside down, and Philip was skinned alive. These men lived out the intensity of this doctrine in their day and hour. Why wouldn't John believe that he was living in the last days?

Jesus said that as the end approached it would be like a woman in labor:

Nation will rise against nation, and kingdom against kingdom. There will be earthquakes in

33

various places, and famines. These are the beginning of birth pains (Mark 13:8, NIV).

The closer a woman gets to delivery, the more intense
her labor pains become. She never quite knows when the
time of delivery will come, but labor pains are a sign that
something is about to happen. Each generation has had
increasing "labor pains."

Jesus used the experience of labor to describe how every
dimension of society would increase in "labor pains" as the
time of delivery drew closer. The earth, He said, would
experience the intensifying pains called earthquakes. Society,
He said, would experience intensifying pains called wars
and famine.

Paul also used the metaphor of labor pains to describe
how the world would be caught off guard at the rapture of
the church (1 Thess. 4:17–5:3). He wrote:

> For when they say, Peace and safety; then sudden
> destruction cometh upon them, as travail upon a
> woman with child; and they shall not escape (5:3).

Increasing Labor Pains

The apostle Paul also wrote, "For we know that the
whole creation groans and labors with birth pangs together
until now" (Rom. 8:22, NKJV). Roberts Liardon writes about
these "birth pangs" in his book *Final Approach*. "The things
we see going on in the world today are the birth pains. As
any woman who has borne children can tell you, those
birth pangs come at the crucial time of transition." He
continues, "We are living in a great time of change from
one era to another. Christians must learn how to survive
victoriously during this time of transition." He concludes by
saying we "are to claim and conquer new territories for God
all over this world until that day comes."[2]

Earthquakes, famines and wars have intensified over the centuries and will continue to do so (1 Thess. 5:3; Mark 13:8; Is. 26:17 – 27:1). Earthquakes, famines and wars have always existed, but not to the degree we see today. Geologists tell us that earthquakes are greater and more intense than at any other time in history. Famines have also increased.[3]

Dr. Lester Sumrall, in his book *Time Bomb in the Middle East — Countdown to Armageddon*, interprets these "labor pains" as signs of judgment. He says, "God will give fair warning that judgment is coming." Sumrall, who has lived during most of this century, addresses the intensifying of these signs, saying, "Just think of how the world has changed since 1900. Knowledge has increased in all areas of life. But, more important has been the spiritual revival that began in 1900 and has swept over the entire world."[4]

What Lester Sumrall is referring to are the labor pains of the Pentecostal movement. A major key to this movement was the doctrine of the second coming, which was rejected by mainline denominational churches prior to the turn-of-the-century. Pentecostals saw that Christ could return at any moment, and the masses responded to the gospel they proclaimed. Tens of thousands of people were swept into the kingdom.

Today we are in the midst of what may be called the "last days revival." More souls are coming into the kingdom now than in any other generation. Church growth experts are constantly revising their worldwide percentages. Carman gives us an interesting statistic: "For the first time in over a thousand years, the majority of Christians are not in the New World (North America and Europe) but in the Third World. The unstoppable gospel is spreading like wildfire all over the world."[5]

This reveals another tension that is present in our generation. On one side we see multitudes coming to Christ as in no other time in the history of Christianity, and on the other side we see Christians growing cold in their relationship with Jesus (Matt. 24:12). Carman notes, "Some are convinced that the end of the world is near because things look really bad. On the other hand, when God is moving everywhere in great power, these conclude that it certainly must be the last great end-time revival."[6]

Benny Hinn shares a powerful revelation the Spirit of the Lord gave Him about end-time revival in his book *The Anointing*. Hinn begins by using Acts 3:19-21 to call us to repentance:

> Repent ye therefore, and be converted, that your sins may be blotted out, when the times of refreshing shall come from the presence of the Lord; And he shall send Jesus Christ, which before was preached unto you: Whom the heaven must receive until the times of restitution of all things, which God hath spoken by the mouth of all his holy prophets since the world began (Acts 3:19-21).

According to Benny Hinn, the words of this passage from Acts indicate that all the prophecies in Scripture regarding restoration will come to pass before the return of the Lord. He then quotes Isaiah 35:1-10 and shows seven areas of restoration in this prophecy.

1. Unprecedented worldwide evangelism, "a worldwide release of the supernatural, a fresh anointing of power."

2. A worldwide release of the supernatural. "I am confident that the day is coming when every believer will be healthy." (Kathryn Kuhlman said the same thing about the last days. See also Ps. 105:37.)

3. A mighty end-time anointing of the baptism of the Holy Spirit (Is. 35:6-7).

4. Deliverance from every demonic influence for God's people (Is. 35:7).

5. Holiness in the body of Christ (Is. 35:8).

6. The absence of Satan and his demons from the body of Christ (Is. 35:9).

7. The rapture of the church (Is. 35:10).[7]

One thing is for certain, this generation is closer to the return of Christ than any previous generation. If the apostle John wrote, "Little children, it is the last time" (1 John 2:18), then it is safe to say that we are living in the last seconds of the last minutes.

For more evidence that we are living in the last days, we will examine in the next chapter what charismatics have to say about the signs of the times.

Practical Application

If we are to apply this truth to our lives, we must live like the writers of the New Testament — with the tension that this is the last generation. Everything we do, whether it be in our ministries or our vocations, should be based on the knowledge that Christ could return at any moment. At the same time we should perform with excellence so that when Christ does return, He will find us faithfully doing what He told us to do.

I have heard more than one person say, "We don't have time to waste on planning, education and erecting buildings. We need to be out preaching." This is fatal thinking. All of these things are necessary to fulfill the plan of God. When I went to Bible college, I led hundreds to Christ through a street ministry. When the church I pastor erected a new building, contractors were touched and workers were saved. God is a God of order and planning. We have to do what He says and leave the rest to Him.

I remember Dr. Larry Lea sharing with us seminary students about the first time he met Dr. Cho. He was given two minutes to ask him anything he wanted. Larry asked Dr. Cho, "How did you build the largest church in all of the history of Christianity?" Dr. Cho replied, "Simple. I prayed, and I obeyed; ha, ha, ha!" That may sound very simplistic, yet it is profoundly practical. When Jesus returns, I want to be found praying and obeying!

5

SIGNS OF THE TIMES

God's Word: The Key to Unlocking the Cryptogram

One of the most prolific Word of Faith teachers over the years has been Charles Capps. Jerry Savelle said at a Southwest Believer's Convention that Charles was one of the most consistent teachers of the Word he knew. Charles ministered a very powerful message on the end times at the church that I pastor. In his message "Signposts Along the Way," Capps said that many believers think the signs of the end times refer to the rapture, when, in fact, most scriptures refer to another event, the second coming.

Capps also said that during the last days of His teaching,

Jesus focused on the rapture and His second coming. Capps used the three accounts in the Synoptic Gospels (Matthew, Mark and Luke), to explore the last days of Christ's life. Even in the giving of communion, Jesus talked about the future kingdom and the marriage supper of the Lamb. Near the close of each of these Gospels we find Jesus addressing the end of the ages and the signs of the times (Matt. 24 – 25; Mark 13; Luke 21).

Capps pointed out that Jesus was addressing a Jewish audience and that the signs were answers to Jewish questions. Since Scripture teaches that masses of Jews will be converted during the tribulation period, Capps said that most of these signs were directed to Jews who will go through the tribulation.[1]

Dave Breese, who has a program on Trinity Broadcasting Network, agrees. Breese says that the only way to discuss the signs of the times is by looking into "God's prophetic Word." He says that God's Word informs us that "Christ's second coming will cast shadows before it."

According to Breese, the next sign we should watch for is the "rapture of the church" (1 Thess. 4:16-17; 2 Thess. 2:1). Breese makes the point correctly that though we "look forward to the *rapture of the church*, we must remember that the signs given to us in Scripture basically apply to the second coming — the return of Christ in power and great glory."[2] Oral Roberts calls these signs of the times "signposts pointing to the imminent return."[3]

Signs in This Present Generation

Today we do not need to sensationalize the events of our day to convince people how close we are to the return of Christ. As you and I read the newspapers or watch the evening news, we realize how late the hour is.

My own conversion came as a result of realizing the signs of the times. Prior to my conversion, I can recall many times both at work and in my social life when this topic came up. Then I was invited to an Assemblies of God church to hear messages on the second coming of Christ. God used that series of messages to bring me to Christ, which is why I believe this to be one of the most evangelistic doctrines of the church. I was aware of the signs of my times.

In the Gospel of Mark, Jesus said:

> Now learn a parable of the fig tree; When her branch is yet tender, and putteth forth leaves, ye know that summer is near: So ye in like manner, when ye shall see these things come to pass, know that it is nigh, even at the doors. Verily I say unto you, that *this generation* shall not pass, till all these things be done (13:28-30, italics added).

This text always troubled me because I had interpreted it incorrectly. If it is interpreted as saying that the generation of the disciples would not pass away until these things came to pass, then the words of Jesus did not come to pass. But that is not what Jesus said. He clearly stated that the generation that sees "these things" come to pass shall not pass away until they are all done. "These things" are the signs of the times.

What Are the Signs of the Times?

So what are the signs of the times? Interpreting Scripture is not complex; the key is context. The context of Jesus' words are the first thirty verses of Mark. This is paralleled in Matthew 24:1-30 where Jesus responds to the questions the disciples pose in verses 1-3.

1. When will the temple be torn down?

2. What will be the sign of Your coming?

41

3. What will be the sign of the end of the ages?

Jesus gave the disciples a brief overview of what the next several generations would experience: wars, rumors of wars, earthquakes in diverse places and famine. Every generation since then has experienced these with increasing intensity. Yet these are only the beginning of the signs.

Roberts Liardon, in his book *Final Approach,* says that these signs are not to trouble us. Jesus said, "See that ye be not troubled: for all these things must come to pass, but the end is not yet" (Matt. 24:6). Liardon adds that when we see these things come to pass, "We should rejoice because it simply means that we are getting closer to the end. We are at the beginning of the end, but the end is not yet. Let's heed Jesus' advice and not be troubled."[4]

Some are tempted to defend apologetically the fact that we are in the last days. But the signs speak for themselves and are obvious. The majority of charismatics do not need to be "pumped up" to believe that we are in the last days.

Dr. Richard Eby, in his book *Didn't You Read My Book?,* says that he needs no "more affirmation nor revelation of the signs of the times than those long ignored by people and nations since the prophets of old and the apostles after Pentecost proclaimed them for our edification in the Holy Scriptures." He states that God has announced the "great Day of the Lord" is at hand.[5]

A common theme in charismatic circles is "God said it, I believe it, and that's good enough for me!" Mike Evans, missionary evangelist, in his book *The Return,* does a quick overview of the prophetic track record of the Bible and comes to a similar conclusion: "The Bible is true. One of the reasons the Bible has stood the test of time is the incredible accuracy of its predictions. Roughly two-thirds of all the prophetic utterances in the Bible have already come to pass. Those that remain in waiting have to do with the end of history as we have known it."[6]

Finis Jennings Dake, author of the *Dake's Annotated Reference Bible*, says that all of the biblical prophecies which need to be fulfilled for the rapture to take place are fulfilled and that the remaining prophecies will be fulfilled throughout the tribulation period. An interesting note on what Dake says about the rapture is that often too much emphasis has been placed on this event when, in reality, it is just "one of the signs of the second coming." Dake believes that the reason for the "signs of the times" is to get our focus on the return of Christ to set up His millennial reign.[7]

The reason we believe we are in the last days is because the Word of God says we are. Theology must be based on Scripture, not on what is happening around us in society. Charismatic theology is balanced by the Word, which it should be.

Once we have interpreted the Word and know what signs to look for, we then turn to our society and identify the signs. From these signs, we should be stirred in our hearts to see the lateness of the hour and to repent. Then we must evangelize our society diligently, with sobriety, sincerity and purity, in patience, sanctification and obedience to Christ (Matt. 24:43-44; 1 Thess. 5:1-9,23; 1 Pet. 1:13; Acts 3:19-21; Phil. 1:10; 1 John 3:1-3; 1 Tim. 6:13-14).

> Seeing then that all these things shall be dissolved, *what manner of persons ought ye to be in all holy conversation and godliness*, Looking for and hasting unto the coming of the day of God, wherein the heavens being on fire shall be dissolved, and the elements shall melt with fervent heat? (2 Pet. 3:11-12, italics added).

Specific Signs of Our Times

In her book *Signs in the Heavens*, Marilyn Hickey addresses our society's infatuation with the signs of the times. "There is a growing awareness of the impending return of Jesus, and His final judgment upon the earth." She adds: "Increasing numbers of people have claimed that we are actually living in the 'last days' of God's dispensation of grace before His judgment, and most Bible scholars are in agreement with that point. How can people be sure that Christ will soon remove believers from the earth in what is called the rapture?"[8]

In this section we will examine what charismatics are saying about specific signs that God has given us to keep us stirred up. Often the church becomes complacent because it lives too close to society. To keep the church aware of the signs of the times, God allows the church to experience some of the trouble which those signs produce. God is also faithful to raise up voices to help us interpret what is going on around us. In this section, we will identify the signposts of past, present and future.

Wars and Rumors of Wars

> And ye shall hear of wars and rumours of wars: see that ye be not troubled: for all these things must come to pass, but the end is not yet (Matt. 24:6).

Aimee Semple McPherson, the founder of the Foursquare denomination, writes in her book *The Second Coming of Christ* that since the time Jesus said there would be "wars and rumours of wars," they have existed. "From the conquest and fall of Jerusalem, 70 A.D., to the warring of the Saxons, and of Napoleon Bonaparte, the French Revolution, the separating of the U.S.A. from Great Britain, down to the last generations where those still living remember the Civil War, between the North and South, the struggle in the Philippines, the Boer war, the Boxer Rebellion, one international upheaval has followed another." [9]

These words of Mrs. McPherson are from our past. How much more can we add to what she has said? The casualties of World War I, World War II and the Vietnam War are greater than the casualties of all other wars of history combined. Iran, Iraq, the Persian Gulf region and the Middle East in general have been a hotbed of wars and will continue to be in spite of all the efforts at peace. Africa as a continent has undergone radical changes with the shedding of much blood, and conflict remains in the former Yugoslavia and the Baltic nations.

Jesus said these are just two of the signs along the way, but He added that when you see these signs come to pass, be not troubled, for the end is not yet (Matt. 24:6-7).

Famine, Pestilence and Earthquakes

All these are the beginning of sorrows (Matt. 24:8).

Oral Roberts, in his book *The Drama of the End Time,* says, "Multiplied millions in our modern times have perished in widespread famines in India, Russia and China. Pestilence usually follows wars and famines. Never in history has humanity as a whole marched as sheep to a slaughter. The picture is very dark, but there is a brighter view."[10]

Nightly we see pictures from nations like Rwanda on our televisions. James Robison's ministry is reaching out to Rwanda. He believes the famine there is one of the greatest in recorded history.

C. M. Ward, the great "Revivaltime" radio host, who is often seen on TBN's "Praise the Lord," wrote an entire work on earthquakes and the end times. He reveals that earthquakes are not new to us, pointing out biblical accounts of earthquakes (Num. 16; Zech. 14:5). A quake in Portugal in

1775 killed sixty thousand people, and others of wide-spread destruction have occurred in Italy, India, San Francisco and Turkey. Nearly one million earthquakes a year jar and disturb [the earth's] structure.[11]

Lester Sumrall, in his book *I Predict 2000 A.D.*, tells us, "In the 16th century there were 115 [earthquakes]. In the 17th century there were 253. In the 18th century there were 378. In the 19th century there were 640. In the 20th century there have already been 2,119 [earthquakes]."[12]

Earthquakes have occurred in previous centuries, but not with the force and loss which we have seen in our lifetime. In recent history, tragedy has struck in various parts of the world, including here in the United States. But, again, Jesus said these were only the beginning of birth pangs.

Increase of Knowledge

> But thou, O Daniel, shut up the words, and seal the book, even to the time of the end: many shall run to and fro, and knowledge shall be increased (Dan. 12:4).

Maria Woodworth-Etter, a well-known female evangelist at the turn of the century, wrote at the end of her life: "When we stop to consider that we have gone from ox carts to flying machines in one generation, and that we have gone from no means of communication except letter and stage coach, to the immense public press, the telephone and telegraph with their ceaseless streams of news and information, and which cover the earth with their ever-increasing circulation, like falling leaves from some mighty tree of knowledge, we can readily see the fulfillment of Daniel's prophecy." Mrs. Etter goes on to say that Daniel's revelation was locked up to the end of the age, and only since the mid-1800s was it unlocked to her generation.[13]

I wonder what Mrs. Woodworth-Etter would say today?

We are in the computer era; we travel the "information superhighway." When the forerunners of the charismatic movement wrote, they spoke of Daniel's prophecies in terms of automobiles, trains and the new flying machines. Today the technology curve is completely off the graph. Pick up a book today on eschatology, such as Peter and Paul Lalonde's book *The Mark of the Beast*, and you will read about microchips, satellites and tracking stations able to track cattle with implanted chips in their ears from thousands of miles away. Daniel's prophecy is upon our generation, and there is no doubt in my heart that this will propel us into the millennium.

False Messiahs

> For many shall come in my name, saying, I am Christ; and shall deceive many (Mark 13:6).

Every generation has had false messiahs arise, but this generation is the first to see one of these false messiahs hold the FBI hostage for weeks on end on international television. David Koresh read the book of Revelation to the world, and we watched innocent children burn alive.

These false christs will come and go until Satan's ultimate false christ, Antichrist, is revealed. He will be one of the last signs before the return of the true Christ.

False Prophets

> And many false prophets shall rise, and shall deceive many (Matt 24:11).

The Hebrew word for "prophet" is the word *nabiy*, and it means "to be a spokesperson for someone. "The false religions of the world have had many false spokespersons. Joseph Smith (Mormonism), Mohammed (Islam), Mary

Baker Eddy (Christian Science) and A. C. Bhaktivedanta, who founded the International Society for Krishna (Hinduism). But the ultimate false prophet will stand as a spokesperson to promote the Antichrist. He will be the false prophet of Revelation 13. Until this false prophet is revealed, there will be a growing number of lesser false prophets in the earth.

Major Apostasy

> Now the Spirit speaketh expressly, that in the latter times some shall depart from the faith, giving heed to seducing spirits, and doctrines of devils (1 Tim. 4:1).

Oral Roberts says that "many who once believed the fundamental doctrines of God's Word have now turned away from the truth. As a result, millions merely profess religion. They have not been called to paths of repentance, nor urged to forsake sin."[14]

Just this week, a person called our offices who had seen a television program we did. This nice lady told me how she had stopped attending her mainline denominational church because they forsook the Bible and embraced homosexuality. This, in my estimation, is the greatest degree of apostasy the church has ever seen.

Many Christians in today's society are just like this lady. They are sheep without shepherds. I thank God for my roots in Pentecostal/charismatic theology, which keep me in line with the Bible. May this be a warning to all of us who minister to stay on the straight and narrow path of the Word.

Increase of Sin

> This know also, that in the last days perilous times shall come. For men shall be lovers of their own

48

selves, covetous, boasters, proud, blasphemers, disobedient to parents, unthankful, unholy, without natural affection, trucebreakers, false accusers, incontinent, fierce, despisers of those that are good (2 Tim. 3:1-3).

Do not be deceived by false world peace. In my lifetime I have watched wickedness increase. Injustice, racism and murder are at all-time highs. Gang violence is out of control in every major city. I went to school in the suburbs of Cleveland, and we had dress codes then. Today they have metal detectors! On a recent ABC *Nightline* news program, it was reported that the average age of inmates has dropped from thirty years old to twenty.

David Wilkerson, founder of Teen Challenge, prophesied these things in his books *The Vision* and *Racing Toward Judgment*. He told us to watch for an increase of pornography on television and an increase of violence in the streets. Dave also called the church to live in holiness in these last days.

I do not believe Dave's words have fallen on deaf ears. I see two directions people can take in the last days. On one hand sin is growing worse, but on the other hand a remnant bride of Christ is growing in holiness. She is being prepared for her master, and she is alive and well on planet Earth.

Love Waxes Cold

And because iniquity shall abound, the love of many shall wax cold (Matt. 24:12).

The world is growing colder, and the church has its greatest opportunity to shine by walking in real love. The last great move of God will be evangelistic, and it will be in holiness. Satan will heat things up since he knows his time is running short (Rev. 12:12). The gap between good and evil will widen. On one side sin will increase and people will callous themselves to it. On the other side the church will rise up and walk in greater power and love than it has ever known.

I do believe a wave of persecution will unite real believers in the last days. Jesus said we would have persecution, but that we were to be of good cheer, for He has overcome the world (John 16:33).

A Cry for World Peace

> For when they shall say, Peace and safety; then sudden destruction cometh upon them, as travail upon a woman with child; and they shall not escape (1 Thess. 5:3).

When Finis Dake wrote in his day, he said there would be a cry for "peace and safety" just before the return of Christ. He did not see this fulfilled in his lifetime. But it seems today that all we hear about is the New World Order, the end of communism and world peace. As I pen this book, Israel is in the midst of attempting to write peace treaties with her neighboring Arab nations, and no one seems to know what will happen next in Russia.

Things have never changed so rapidly as they are changing today. The bringing down of the Berlin wall and the breakup of communism in the former Soviet Union happened so fast it shocked the world. Stability is a thing of the past. One day they say, "peace and safety," and the next day they experience sudden destruction, like a woman giving birth to a child.

I am a member of Rotary International. Several weeks ago our club invited a high-ranking official from the Ministry of Agriculture in Moscow to speak at our meeting. He and an entire delegation were in our Midwest community to study the free market approach to farming which the former Soviet Union is presently trying to incorporate. He explained that there are many difficulties in his country today as they try to convert to a free market society. I was able to ask a question, and I will never forget the answer nor the look on the official's face. I asked, "What if the free market system doesn't work?" He responded, "It has to work." The words were spoken with great fear as if he knew it wasn't going to work. The former Soviet Union is very volatile as it stands now. Peace and safety are only a smoke cloud in front of what is really happening today. Prophetically, the former Soviet Union is not out of the picture.

Israel Established as a Nation

> And say unto them, Thus saith the Lord God;
> Behold, I will take the children of Israel from
> among the heathen, whither they be gone, and will
> gather them on every side, and bring them into
> their own land: And I will make them one nation
> in the land upon the mountains of Israel; and one
> king shall be king to them all: and they shall be no
> more two nations, neither shall they be divided
> into two kingdoms any more at all (Ezek. 37:21-22).

The nation of Israel was divided into two kingdoms after the death of Solomon, and it was not sovereignly united as a nation until 1948.

Let us not forget the fulfillment of this great Bible prophecy. Israel becoming a nation was at the beginning of what might be called "this generation." Remember that Jesus said that the generation which sees "these things" come to pass shall not pass away until they are all done (Mark 13:30).

Persecution of the Jews

> Then let them which are in Judea flee to the mountains; and let them which are in the midst of it depart out; and let not them that are in the countries enter thereinto (Luke 21:21).

Again, events are happening so fast that we catch ourselves forgetting about the persecutions of the Jews in this century and centuries past. God is not finished with the Jewish people. They have suffered greatly for being God's chosen people, and God promised to graft them back into His plan (Rom. 11:11-32). This is another sign which will not be fulfilled until the tribulation period. Remember the command to pray for the peace of Jerusalem (Ps. 122:6).

End-Time Revival

> Be patient, then, brothers, until the Lord's coming. See how the farmer waits for the land to yield its valuable crop and how patient he is for the autumn and spring rains (James 5:7, NIV).

With everything in my being I believe we are in a worldwide revival. Manifestations of joy are but the beginning of what God is doing. There are "John the Baptists" now sitting on the backsides of the deserts whom God will bring forth in these last days. They will not be the popular voices of the past, but they will take the world by storm. We have planted of our "seeds," and the rains of worldwide revival are upon us. We shall see the great harvest which was prophesied (Acts 2:16-21; Rev. 7:9-17). This sign will not be fulfilled completely until the second coming. Many souls will be saved during the tribulation period.

The Gospel Being Preached in All the World

> And this gospel of the kingdom shall be preached
> in all the world for a witness unto *all nations;* and
> then shall the end come (Matt. 24:14, italics added).

Some would debate whether this sign has been fulfilled or
not. A closer look at this text reveals that it has been fulfilled.

Jesus said that the gospel was to be preached in all the
world as a witness to "all nations." The Greek word for
"nations" is the word *ethnos* from which we derive the word
ethnic. Ethnos means "a race, nation or people" and is a
general reference for the expression "heathen."

I know of no nation on the earth in which the gospel has
not been preached. Jesus did not say that every person
would hear the gospel, but He said that the gospel would
be preached in every nation, and then the end would come.
According to world missions reports I have seen and heard,
the gospel is being preached all over this world as in no
other time in the history of mankind. Just this week I
received a letter from Van Crouch Ministries quoting Dr. D.
James Kennedy as stating that "92,000 people per day from
around the world are coming into the kingdom of God."

As in the Days of Noah

> And as it was in the days of Noe [Noah], so shall it
> be also in the days of the Son of man. They did
> eat, they drank, they married wives, they were
> given in marriage, until the day that Noe entered
> into the ark, and the flood came, and destroyed
> them all (Luke 17:26-27).

No matter how many of these signs are revealed, the
world will still act like the world. Satan blinds those who do

not want to hear and see the obvious. When Jesus returns for the church, it will be life as usual for those left behind, or so they think. "Sudden destruction" shall overtake this world unexpectedly. That is why Jesus told us to watch and wait.

Scoffers

Knowing this first, that there shall come in the last days scoffers, walking after their own lusts, and saying, Where is the promise of his coming? for since the fathers fell asleep, all things continue as they were from the beginning of the creation (2 Pet. 3:3-4.)

Every generation has its scoffers, so they should not affect the way a Christian believes. Peter, under the inspiration of the Holy Spirit, warns every generation not to listen to those who question why we believe Jesus will return. We are told to be ready to give an answer for the reason for our hope (1 Pet. 3:15; Col. 4:6). I cannot think of a better response than to point a scoffer to the signs of the times, and then to lead him to the cross!

The Revival of the Roman Empire

And the ten horns out of this kingdom are ten kings that shall arise: and another shall rise after them; and he shall be diverse from the first, and he shall subdue three kings (Dan. 7:24).

This is one of the signs of the times which we are still waiting to see completely fulfilled. Over the years we have seen partial fulfillment of this text, but not even the European Common Market has exactly ten nations in it right now. This prophecy could be fulfilled either before or after the rapture.

Signs also have another purpose. Jesus said knowing the signs of the times would prepare us for what is coming. If the body of Christ ever needed to be prepared, it is now. In the next chapter we will discuss how to *prepare!*

Practical Application

Signs are given to show direction. Use the Word of God to understand the signs of the times. Stay in tune with what is happening in the world. God has placed these signs around us to use as tools, to show people that the Word is relevant in their lives.

The newspaper reads like pages out of the Bible. When President Clinton met with the prime minister of Israel, Yitzhak Rabin, and Mr. Arafat of the Palestine Liberation Organization for the historic signing of their peace treaty, I held up before my congregation the front page of our local newspaper in one hand and the Bible in my other hand. "When they say peace and safety," I declared, "then comes sudden destruction" (1 Thess. 5:3). Then I asked them the question, "What do you think the front page will look like when the Antichrist signs his peace agreement with Israel?" (Dan. 9:24-27).

As ministers of the Word we have a responsibility to make it relevant to the lives of our people. God has designed the Word to be lived out prophetically in every society. You must find those pages and share them in ways that will cause those around you to stop and think, The Bible really is true! (see 1 Pet. 3:15).

6

PREPARE!

How to Build an Ark of Protection

Christ's thrust in teaching about His second coming was that His people be prepared. Jesus' end-time parable about the ten virgins (Matt. 25:1-13) focused on preparation. Five of the virgins were prepared, and five were not. Also, Jesus' reference to His return as a thief in the night (Matt. 24:42-44) reinforces the idea of readiness.

In his tremendous work *Parables,* Jamie Buckingham wrote an entire chapter on the "Parable of the Five Foolish Maidens." He pointed out that although all ten virgins had oil to start with, "It's not enough to be a Christian. You need the reserve of the Holy Spirit as well."

Buckingham said God will arrive according to His time, not ours. It may be midnight. "Your task is to wait — and be prepared." He added that the church is entering a time of crisis, and we must be prepared to face the outcome of future events. We need spiritual reserves.

"The wise man knows the benefit of filling himself with God's Word in good times so that when bad times come he will be prepared." He concluded: "God loves us enough to shake us to see if there's any oil left in the bottom of our lamps. Nighttime is coming, Jesus indicated. Now, while it is still day, is the time to fill up with reserves. The oil of spiritual power is hard to come by at midnight."[1]

Rodney Howard-Browne, in his book *The Touch of God*, also calls the church to prepare, saying: "In these last days there will be those who will say, 'Where is the sign of His coming?' Let me tell you, He is coming! He wants you to be ready and the only way you are going to be ready is to be full of the oil of the Holy Ghost." Howard-Browne continues: "Do you want to be caught with your lamp empty? If you are not going for God, you are going against Him. If you are cold in your life and can't read your Bible, or you can't pray, or you can't worship God, then there is something wrong. You need the oil of the Holy Ghost to come into your life."[2]

Gloria Copeland has written an entire book on the subject of being ready and prepared. In *Build Yourself an Ark* she says, "In the days ahead you're going to see a great deal of trouble in the world around you. Things on this earth are going to get worse, just like they did in Noah's day." Then Gloria Copeland gives us this warning, "Don't wait until trouble hits to start building your ark, because you want to have it finished before trouble comes."[3]

The way we build an ark is by daily being in the Word and meditating until our spirits are filled with the promises of God. You must remember that no matter how cold and dark the world becomes in the last days, you have the promise that you are children of the day. You are not appointed to wrath. That day shall not come upon you as a thief in the night, but you will be delivered in the "ark" of Christ, the rapture of the church (1 Thess. 5:4-9).

Gloria Copeland points out that Noah was not in darkness when trouble hit, like those in unbelief were. She says, "Noah wasn't in the dark — he was in the ark!"[4] That's where you and I need to be when trouble hits — in the ark!

Beware of Deception

Dr. David Yonggi Cho, in his book *Prayer: Key to Revival*, calls us to preparation with a strong warning about deception in the last days. He says that as we approach the last days we must beware of false prophets. "Satan will try to deceive the church with many voices. Yet, those who learn to listen to God will not be deceived because they will know the difference between God speaking and counterfeit voices." Dr. Cho refers to Matt. 24:37-39:

> But as the days of Noe [Noah] were, so shall also the coming of the Son of man be. For as in the days that were before the flood they were eating and drinking, marrying and giving in marriage, until the day that Noe entered into the ark, and knew not until the flood came, and took them all away; so shall also the coming of the Son of man be.

Dr. Cho says that, as in the days of Noah, the world today is not conscious of the times or signs of His coming. We see people today totally unaware of the lateness of the hour. We as believers must heed the advice of Dr. Cho to stay in communion with God and learn to listen to the voice of the

Holy Spirit preparing us for what is ahead.[5]

Another charismatic with a strong warning about preparation is David Wilkerson. Wilkerson, in his book *Racing Toward Judgment*, says, "Don't be caught unaware." He writes of hearing God say to him, "Prepare to meet God." God told him to share the message of preparation with his generation. He believes that many Christians are not prepared to meet God. "They are not prepared for the coming of Christ or impending judgment."[6]

In Jesus' discourse in Matthew 24 He warns the believer that one of the signs of the end times is deception (Matt. 24:4-5,11,23-26). Francis Frangipane, a young prophet/teacher in the charismatic movement with a message of repentance and a call to unity, warns the body of Christ of the deadliness of the deception found in religion. In his book *Holiness, Truth, and the Presence of God*, Frangipane says, "Remaining free from deception is a responsibility each of us must assume as individuals." He continues by saying if we are not careful to examine what we are taught, we will fall into the deception of dead religion.[7]

The apostle Paul, inspired by the Holy Spirit, writes and warns us in 2 Timothy 3 of what the last days will be like:

> This know also, that in the last days perilous times
> shall come...men having a form of godliness, but
> denying the power thereof (vv. 1-2,5).

Dr. John Avanzini says of this passage of Scripture that if Paul warned the early church to be careful and guard itself against satanic religious deceptions, "How much more you and I must be vigilant in our watch in today's society!"[8]

Charismatics have been accused of having no accountability in the area of doctrine, but this could not be further from the truth. It is my experience that among charismatics there is a constant call to beware of deception. Charismatic theology is sound in that the believer is consistently called to study the Scriptures (2 Tim. 2:15).

Many voices inside the charismatic movement are calling the church to prepare for the second coming of Christ. One such voice is a young pastor named Rod Parsley from Columbus, Ohio. He wrote an entire book on preparation, *Tribulation to Triumph*. During a quiet time, the Spirit of God led him to Luke 21:6, in which Jesus responded to His disciples' desire to know what sign He would give concerning His return.

> Days will come, in which there shall not be left one stone upon another, that shall not be thrown down.

Parsley interprets this text in light of the historical fulfillment of the events of A.D. 70. Historians tell us that at that time Rome destroyed Jerusalem and tore down the temple stone by stone. Then Parsley challenges charismatic believers that God in these last days is preparing the church. He says we believers must check our foundations to see if what we have built upon is the revelation of Christ or our own works.[9] He is right in his assessment of the passage, for Paul writes that whatever is not of Christ will be burned up on that day (1 Cor. 3:10-15).

Preparing the Bride With Prophecy

Several years ago the Lord spoke to me about a young prophetic psalmist named Lori Wilke. When I first heard Lori, God spoke to my heart to have Lori minister every year in our church. I believe that God brings ministry gifts such as prophecy to churches to mature the church body (Eph. 4:8-14).

In her book *The Costly Anointing*, Lori says that the prophetic ministry is preparing the bride of Christ. "This preparation is a washing of water by the word to remove spots, wrinkles and blemishes, while giving great comfort to the church in the glorious hope of Jesus' second return." The book of Titus describes what Christians should do as they wait for Jesus' second coming.

> Teaching us that, denying ungodliness and worldly lusts, we should live soberly, righteously, and godly, in this present world; looking for that blessed hope, and the glorious appearing of the great God and our Saviour Jesus Christ (Titus 2:12-13).

Lori writes, "The plan of God's heart is to return for a people who are mature and have become mighty in spirit in this present world." She adds, "This prophetic ministry challenges God's people to step out of infancy and into a state of responsibility."[10] Jesus referred to this responsibility in the parable of the ten pounds, adding, "Occupy till I come" (Luke 19:13).

Another young prophet calling the bride to prepare for Christ's return is Kim Clement from South Africa. He says that the reward for those who overcome is a garment without spot (Rev. 3:3-4). "We are fast approaching the hour that has been described as the conflict of the ages. Without question we are going to see the things of the Lord being duplicated by false apostles, false teachers and false prophets as never before."

Clement adds: "At the same time we will see a victorious outburst of God's expression on the earth — and you and I will participate in it. Truth will swallow up evil. The power of God will be unprecedented, and we will be ushered into a land that knows no defilement."[11]

Rodney Howard-Browne tells us the bride must be ready. "I am telling you, there is a cry in the Spirit that says, 'Behold, the bridegroom cometh.' He is coming! He is coming! It does not matter what you believe or what your theology is. He is coming! He is not waiting for you to make up your mind and say, 'Okay, Lord, You can come now.' He is coming!" [12]

Practical Application

We are responsible to keep ourselves ready for the return of Christ. Each of us must develop the joy of disciplining ourselves in prayer and the daily reading of the Word. I cannot stress enough the need to build up one's spiritual reserves. With each approaching day we will need more anointing. The hour to build the ark is not when the storm hits, but now.

We also need corporate responsibility. We should not forsake assembling together, especially as we see the day approaching. Rodney Howard-Browne reminds us of the need to be in church. "Don't ever say that you can make it without your brothers and sisters. Don't ever say that you don't need to go to church." Howard-Browne writes:

> Some people miss church, saying, It is the only time we have to spend with the family. But the Bible says, "Not forsaking the assembling of ourselves together, as the manner of some is; but exhorting one another: and so much the more, as ye see the day approaching" (Heb. 10:25). The day of Christ's return is approaching! We are closer today than we have ever been. There is an urgency in my spirit, the clock is ticking away and there is a job to be done.[13]

There is also a real need in the church for balance. The five-fold ministry (apostles, prophets, evangelists, pastors and teachers) must be active in each church. That does not mean that we need to have all five offices present all the time. It does mean that we need to be in relationship with the five-fold ministry. We can do this by inviting guest speakers who are called into these various areas. We need them, and they need us.

One of the most neglected ministries I see is the office of the prophet. God has and still is raising a generation of John the Baptists. Some of them are still in the wilderness, but God is ready to unleash them on the church to prepare for His return.

7

THE PREMILLENNIAL RETURN OF CHRIST

The Major Charismatic Position

While the doctrine concerning the rapture of the church varies among believers, the vast majority of charismatics believe in the premillennial return of Christ. Strong unity exists within charismatic theology that Jesus will return before the beginning of the millennium, or the one thousand year reign of Christ (Rev. 20:2-4). This is known as the premillennial return of Christ.

Dr. David Yonggi Cho, in his book *Revelation*, says, "Revelation 19-20 tells us that when the last day of the earth comes near, after the battle of Armageddon, Jesus will come

64

down to the earth accompanied by a multitude of His saints." Cho says that at that time Christ will defeat His enemies and will then reign with His saints for one thousand years (the millennium).[1]

Marilyn Hickey writes on this subject in her book *Armageddon*. She declares that we are winners at Armageddon! "God's righteous — Christians and all the Jews who believe Jesus is their Messiah — will receive the title deed to the earth. They will live without evil in their midst." Marilyn says they will be a part of God's divine process to restore the world back to paradise during the millennium.[2]

Another charismatic Bible teacher who believes in the premillennial return of Christ is Hilton Sutton. In his book *Rapture: Get Right or Get Left*, he states that we should be excited about the soon return of Jesus to establish His kingdom on earth. "The prophecies of Isaiah 9:6 will be fulfilled: the government shall be upon His shoulder." But, Sutton says, before Jesus can establish His millennial reign, two major events must take place. These two events are His appearing and His return.[3]

Before the Millennium

I believe that Dr. Cho, Marilyn Hickey and Hilton Sutton are correct in their assessments that the return of Christ will be before the beginning of the millennial reign of Christ in the earth. In Revelation 19 – 22 the events are written in chronologically correct order. In Revelation 19 we see the second coming of Christ with the saints of God and the defeat of the Antichrist and the false prophet (vv. 11-21). Then we see in chapter 20 that Satan is bound by an angel for one thousand years, and Christ's earthly reign is established. The chronology of these texts give strong support to the charismatic premillennial position.

Other Millennial Positions

There are several other theological positions concerning the return of Christ in relationship to His millennial reign. These schools of thought are the result of different approaches to interpreting Revelation 20:1-6, the most significant passage on the millennium.

Postmillennial

The postmillennial position says that Jesus will return at the end of the millennium. Postmillennialists contend that we are presently in the millennium.

The postmillennial school focuses greatly on scripture verses in which metaphors are used. For example, Jesus said that the kingdom of God is like yeast (Matt. 13:33; Luke 13:20-21). A postmillennialist would immediately say that this means we are presently in the millennium and that the kingdom of God is going to take a thousand years to work itself into every area of society and eventually take over the world so that good conquers evil.

Similar interpretations are made of the parable of the sower (Matt. 13:1-9; Mark 4:1-20; Luke 8:4-15), the parable of weeds among wheat (Matt. 13:24-30,37-43) and the parable of the dragnet (Matt. 13:47-50). In the parable of the sower, the postmillennialist says that the seed is the kingdom, and ultimately it will take over the world. In reality the seed is the Word and works only in those who hear and obey (Matt. 13:23).

In both the parable of the weeds and the parable of the dragnet, scriptures are interpreted by postmillennialists to say evil is overcome gradually by good. But Jesus was referring to a day of judgment when angels would be called upon to separate the children of God from the children of Satan. In order to preserve their point of view, liberal postmillennialists have to ignore statements from Jesus such as, "The love of many shall wax cold [in the end times]" (Matt. 24:12).

A postmillennial charismatic would believe that we are presently in the millennium or about to usher it in, and when we have finished "possessing the land," we will bring about the second coming of Christ. This group of charismatics are called kingdom-now, or dominionist, believers. In other words, they believe that the kingdom of God has arrived, and we are presently ruling and reigning with Christ.

Hal Lindsey, a frequent guest and host of Trinity Broadcasting Network's "Praise the Lord" program, wrote a book attempting to warn the charismatic movement of the dangers of postmillennial eschatology. Lindsey shows a "marriage" of the charismatics to the evangelical reconstructionism. The only problem is that the marriage never took place! Lindsey defined evangelical reconstructionism as the belief that Christians have the mandate from God to reconstruct society by strictly instituting the civil code of the law of Moses over the governments of the world.[4]

In the twelve chapters of *The Road to Holocaust*, Lindsey quotes only one prolific charismatic who bought into postmillennial thinking — Earl Paulk, a pastor from Atlanta who wrote *To Whom Is God Betrothed?* Paulk did cause the charismatic camps to rethink this area of theology, but made no lasting impact on the solid premillennial position.[5]

Another major charismatic personality who adopted this thinking was Pastor Thomas Reid from Buffalo, New York. However, Reid took the kingdom-now teaching and kept it in balance with his premillennial theology. He writes that "many kingdom-now teachers remain, as I do, premillennialists. They maintain their belief in a rapture, tribulation, Armageddon and the millennial reign." Reid continues by saying that this teaching has impacted him and others not to sit around fatalistically and wait for the rapture, but rather to involve themselves in society and possess the land through Christ. He concludes: "Theology of dominion does not destroy any particular eschatological position. One can believe in a pretribulation rapture and a premillennial return of Christ and still hold to an escha- tology of dominion. The final conflict will not be the result of an anemic church being rescued at the very end, but rather the conflict created by the power of a church in the midst of revival influencing all the world."[6]

It is important to explain what the kingdom-now/re- construction camp was trying to say. Hal Lindsey correctly quotes an acquaintance of mine, Dr. H. Wayne House, who was an adjunct professor at Oral Roberts University while I was a graduate fellow studying for my masters of divinity. Dr. House wrote a book after leaving ORU which correctly assesses the reconstruction and postmillennial situation.

In his work *Dominion Theology: Blessing or Curse?*, Dr. House ties American history in with church history by explaining that the Puritans came to this country to estab- lish religious freedom and a "new world" based on the Old Testament civil code called the Law. Those who possess the view of end-time theology that the "kingdom is here" must involve themselves in civil government, "possessing the land" so Jesus can return.[7]

This becomes a very complex issue not only for charismatics, but for all believers because we believe it is God's will to possess the land. In fact, if anybody bought into postmillennial thinking, it was not the charismatics, but rather the evangelicals, and it is not difficult to see why. Dr. House, who is an evangelical, writes about those who call themselves Christian reconstructionists and propose to institute a theocratic (godly) government in America, and they are gaining support in some elements of the evan- gelical community.[8]

The error in this thinking is the belief that man's efforts

can create a perfect government which will usher the return of Christ. In reality Jesus said that everything would get worse, and the love of many would grow cold (Matt. 24:12). Again, it cannot be stressed enough that the vast majority of charismatics are premillennialists who believe that when Jesus returns to the earth He will return to a "cataclysmic judgment of the whole world."[9] Yet, at the same time, we do believe that we have a responsibility to be involved in every field of life including government and that we are to "possess the land" until Jesus comes. The church is to be a preserving agent in the earth. Jesus said:

> Ye are the salt of the earth: but if the salt have lost his savour, wherewith shall it be salted? it is thenceforth good for nothing, but to be cast out, and to be trodden under foot of men. Ye are the light of the world. A city that is set on a hill cannot be hid. Neither do men light a candle, and put it under a bushel, but on a candlestick; and it giveth light unto all that are in the house. Let your light so shine before men, that they may see your good works, and glorify your Father which is in heaven (Matt. 5:13-16).

A Strong Warning From the Past

Finis Jennings Dake, one of the most outstanding theological thinkers of his day and the author of the *Dake's Annotated Reference Bible* offers us a strong warning about postmillennial theology. Dake says the doctrine of the apostles was premillennial, and it remained the church's doctrine until the third century when a theologian named Origen "spiritualized" the Word. From that time on, "Many ceased to believe in a literal return and an earthly reign of Christ."

Dake says that not until the Reformation was the biblical

concept of a literal millennium restored. He adds, "The theory of postmillennialism is dangerous and unscriptural. It would have us substitute man and his works for the work of God. It would have us believe that man is going to usher in his own millennium and secure his own happiness by his own efforts."[10]

Lest we should unfairly condemn the postmillennial school, C. P. Nelson says that this was a widely held school of thought until about 1900. Today, the premillennial school of thought is the main evangelical position; however, it was not always popular. The majority of theologians at the turn of the century held to the postmillennial position and scorned those who said otherwise. C. P. Nelson says that "Charles Spurgeon, Dwight L. Moody, Wilbur Chapman, A. J. Gordon, A. B. Simpson and others who would not accept this [postmillennial] teaching were considered peculiar, and their teaching was dangerous."[11] All of these men were premillennialists.

The focus of postmillennial teaching is on victory and triumph, and is therefore attractive to some. However, it depends on a needlessly symbolic interpretation of Revelation 20, which says that Satan will be bound in chains for a thousand years. Since the postmillennialist believes we are in the millennium, they interpret this to mean that Satan has been restricted in his activities. But those who maintain a high view of the inspiration of Scripture see no need to interpret it in any other way but literally. Satan is clearly not bound or restricted in the present affairs of humanity.

A literal interpretation of Revelation 20 leads to premillennialism. That is why the vast majority of charismatics are premillennialists, not postmillennialists. Also, it should be noted that one of the strengths of charismatic theology is that while we believe in a premillennial return of Christ, we have not become fatalists. Some contemporary non-charismatic theologians have become very pessimistic in their views, thinking there is no hope for victory in this present life. Charismatic theology, though, agrees with Scripture: "We are more than conquerors" through Christ Jesus (Rom. 8:37).

Amillennial

The last position to examine concerning the return of Christ in relationship to the millennium is the amillennial school of thought. I do not know of any published charismatic who is an amillennialist or, in other words, who does not believe in a literal millennium.

The first major proponent of this concept was Augustine (A.D. 354-425). Dr. John Walvoord, an evangelical theologian writes, "Augustine advanced the theory that the thousand years [the millennium] will fall in the interadvent period and will terminate with the second coming."[12]

In other words, Augustine believed that the millennium was a thousand-year period that began at the cross and would end at the second coming. Augustine began as a premillennialist, but due to the carnal nature of those who held to such a belief in his day, he turned against it, spiritualizing Revelation 20. Obviously, that one-thousand-year period came and went (A.D. 32-1032), which made amillennialism a rather unpopular belief after A.D. 1032. Walvoord further states that understanding Augustine's position is important because his views are still the basis for all positions other than premillennialism.[13]

In closing this section it is very important to note that all the major charismatic prophecy teachers are premillennialists who believe in a literal millennial reign of Christ. These teachers agree with and quote mainline evangelical prophecy teachers.

Practical Application

To avoid the premillennial position is to accept another. This means you must either believe there is no millennium, or you must believe that we are already in it. To believe that we are in the millennium means that the devil is already bound, and if the devil is bound, then there is no need for spiritual warfare or resisting temptation.

Believing in any position other than a literal millennial reign of Christ means that you must spiritualize, allegorize or in some other way violate a whole host of scriptures, especially Revelation 20. Then you will have to spend time defending your position (or error). We do not have time for such foolishness. We should be possessing the land, making the kingdoms of this world into the kingdom of our God through evangelism.

8

THE RAPTURE
OF THE CHURCH

The Question Is, When?

As we open the discussion about the rapture of the church, it is important to note that I know of no charismatic teachers who do not believe in the rapture. I also want to be quick to say that while this is true, charismatics are all over the board about when this event will take place and how many times it will occur. For example, Hilton Sutton, in his book *Rapture: Get Right or Get Left*, mentions seven raptures: the raptures of Enoch, Elijah, Jesus, the church, the midtribulation saints, the 144,000 Jews and the two witnesses.[1]

73

Hilton Sutton is a well-known charismatic Bible teacher whose focus is eschatology. He says that he has yet to meet a believer who does not believe in the rapture. In the introduction to his book Sutton says there are some who teach that the word *rapture* is not found in Scripture. But the word *trinity* is not found in Scripture either, yet we all hold to that idea. *Rapture* and *trinity* are terms used for concepts that are biblical. As Sutton points out, "The Bible does talk about our being 'caught up' or 'gathered together unto the Lord,' or Jesus 'receiving us to Himself.'"[2]

Is the Term *Rapture* a Biblical Concept?

Charismatics are quick to acknowledge that the term *rapture* has no root in the Greek, though the concept is biblical. Oral Roberts, in his book *God's Timetable for the End Time!*, says that although the term is not used in the Bible, the rapture, or the mass exodus of believers from the earth, could take place at any moment.[3]

Jack Van Impe, an evangelical Baptist, agrees, pointing out that the word *rapio,* from which we get the English word *rapture* is not in the Bible because it is Latin. But the term rapture was coined to describe a biblical experience. Van Impe is not a charismatic, but his program on the Trinity Broadcasting Network has influenced charismatic believers. He continues, "The term *rapio* means a snatching away."[4]

Bob Yandian, senior pastor of Grace Fellowship and the former dean of instructors at Rhema Bible Training Center, says it is true that the word *rapture* does not appear in the Bible. But he adds, "The concept is still found no matter what it is called. We in the church have appropriated the word from the Latin and applied it to the future 'catching up' or 'rescuing' of the believers."[5]

Scriptural Basis for the Rapture

The following host of passages will develop the biblical concept of the rapture. The first text comes from Paul's letter to a group of new converts at Thessalonica.

> For this we say unto you by the word of the Lord, that we which are alive and remain unto the coming of the Lord shall not prevent [go before] them which are asleep. For the Lord himself shall descend from heaven with a shout, with the voice of the archangel, and with the trump of God: and the dead in Christ shall rise first: Then we which are alive and remain shall be *caught up* together with them in the clouds, to meet the Lord in the air: and so shall we ever be with the Lord (1 Thess. 4:15-17, italics added).

In this text we find the Greek expression *harpazo*, meaning "to seize, to catch (away, up), to pluck, pull or to take out, even by force."

Roy Hicks, in his book *Another Look at the Rapture*, says the expression "caught up" used here is the Greek word *harpazo*, meaning "to be snatched away by a swift, resistless, divine energy." "No matter what word we use — whether rapture, caught, or snatched — it will not change the meaning of the passage." Dr. Hicks makes the point that the text still says we shall be caught up in the air and meet the Lord.[6]

Marilyn Hickey says that the same concept as *harpazo* is found in an Old Testament expression used to describe the event of the rapture. "The same idea of a physical rescue is expressed by Daniel" in his prophecy in chapter 12:

> There shall be a time of trouble, such as never was since there was a nation even to that same time:

75

and at that time thy people shall be delivered, every one that shall be found written in the book (Dan. 12:1, italics added).[7]

The Hebrew word for "delivered" is *malat,* and it means "to escape, to release, to rescue, or to bring forth speedily."

The second passage that develops the biblical concept of the rapture is found in 1 Corinthians 15:

Behold, I shew you a mystery; We shall not all sleep, but we shall all be changed, In a *moment,* in the twinkling of an eye, at the last trump: for the trumpet shall sound, and the dead shall be raised incorruptible, and we shall be changed (vv. 51-52, italics added).

This text reveals two biblical expressions relating to the rapture. In the first phrase, "in a moment, in the twinkling of an eye," Paul uses the Greek word *atomos,* translated here as "moment." We get the word *atom,* or small indivisible part, from that Greek word. Literally, the apostle is saying that in an atomic second, this event shall occur. In an atomic second, millions of believers shall be changed, literally transformed. This event is the rapture.

Marilyn Hickey agrees that this event will happen incredibly fast. "Imagine a measure of time that is so fast that it couldn't be any faster — much like the speed of light. The rapture of the church is even faster."[8]

The second expression used in 1 Corinthians 15:52 is what Paul says will happen during this atomic second. Not only will we be transformed, but we will be *raised.* Here, the Greek word is *egiro,* which means "to awaken, or arise from sleep, from sitting, from lying or from death." This expression is also translated "to lift up, raise up or to take up"!

Keep in mind as we go through these texts that together

76

these descriptions define the theological expression which we will call the rapture. In our next text we see two of the most common expressions used for the concept of the rapture.

> Now we beseech you, brethren, by the *coming* of our Lord Jesus Christ, and by our *gathering together* unto him, That ye be not soon shaken in mind, or be troubled, neither by spirit, nor by word, nor by letter as from us, as that the day of Christ is at hand (2 Thess. 2:1-2, italics added).

The Greek word in this text that is the most commonly used when describing the rapture is the word *parousia,* meaning "to return." The fuller meaning of *parousia* is "to come" in a physical sense, meaning one's literal presence or arrival.

We also find Paul talking about our "gathering together" to Jesus at His physical return. The Greek expression used here, *episunagoge,* means "to assemble or gather together," for example, in a Christian worship meeting. What an assembly that will be!

The fourth passage that helps build a biblical model for the concept of the rapture is in 2 Peter 3:

> Knowing this first, that there shall come in the *last* days scoffers, walking after their own lusts, and saying, Where is the promise of his coming? for since the fathers fell asleep, all things continue as they were from the beginning of the creation (vv. 3-4, italics added).

From this text we get the theological expression "eschatology," or the study of end times. Peter says that in the last (*eschatos*) days scoffers will ask, "Where is the coming (*parousia,* or return) of the Lord?" The answer is

77

clearly that His coming or return, shall be in the clouds at that gathering (1 Thess. 4:17; 2 Thess. 2:1-2).

Our last passage of Scripture is given simply as a word of encouragement to us all:

> Be patient therefore, brethren, unto the *coming* of the Lord...Be ye also patient; stablish your hearts; for the coming of the Lord draweth nigh (James 5:7-8, italics added).

Rev. Kenneth E. Hagin and Dr. Roy Hicks combined their efforts to edit and reprint the work of Dr. T. J. McCrossan, *Bodily Healing and the Atonement.* In this book McCrossan discusses the Greek word *parousia,* translated "coming" in the text above: "The word literally means 'being with' or 'presence.'" McCrossan cites 2 Peter 3:3-4 and 1 Thessalonians 4:15-17, saying that the expression Paul uses, "in the last days," refers to the time just before the *parousia,* or the coming of Christ for His saints (the rapture). McCrossan says, "The dead saints are to rise and be caught up with the saints at the *parousia.*"[9] He is identifying the event known as the rapture.

Billy Graham, in his book *World Aflame,* defines *parousia* as that which carries with it the idea of personal appearance or "the presence of Christ." Graham says, "When Christ comes He will come in person."[10]

When charismatics refer to the rapture, we are referring to the combined concept of the aforementioned scriptures. It is critical to mention that if we are going to teach on the rapture we must distinguish between it and the second coming, as God clearly did in His Word.

Comparing the Rapture and the Second Coming

The rapture of the church and the second coming of Christ are two separate events. While concluding this, it is critical not to take biblical texts out of context to make a point. As we examine the following texts within their given context, it should become clear that we are dealing with two separate and distinct events.

Oral Roberts in his commentary on the New Testament addresses our first text. Concerning the second coming of Christ, Roberts says, "We believe the Bible teaches that He is first coming for His people, and then afterward, He is coming back with those people." Oral identifies the first event as the rapture and the second as the "revelation of Christ," otherwise known as the second coming.[11]

One of the clearest passages of Scripture which identifies the rapture is in Matthew 24:

> So shall also the coming of the Son of man be. Then shall two be in the field; the one shall be taken, and the other left. Two women shall be grinding at the mill; the one shall be taken, and the other left (vv. 39-41).

Dr. Roberts identifies the rapture in this text. "There will be men and women working together. One will be taken up in the rapture, the translation of the saints of God. The other will be left to face the tribulation."[12]

Aimee Semple McPherson agreed. In her book *The Second Coming of Christ*, she said that the second coming will be divided into two parts:

1. His coming *for* His people (1 Thess. 4:17).

2. His coming with His people (Deut. 33:2; Rev. 19:14).

Mrs. McPherson stated, "When Jesus comes *for* His people, His appearance is likened unto a bright and morning star." But she added, "When He comes *with* His people, He shall arise as the Sun of Righteousness with healing in His wings." Concerning these two events she concluded: "When He comes for His people, only the waiting saints will see Him in the air. When He returns bringing His saints with Him, every eye shall see Him, weeping and consternation shall fill the hearts of those who rejected Him."[13]

Dake, who like McPherson was a forerunner and influencer of the charismatic/Pentecostal movement, said the same thing, only more aggressively. "The rapture is also called 'the coming of the Lord' but not His coming to the earth, for He does not come to the earth at this time." Dake added: "The rapture is when Christ comes *for* His saints (1 Thess. 4:13-16). The second coming is when He comes back *with* them (Rev. 19:11-15, Jude 14, Zech. 14:5).

"The rapture takes place *before* the tribulation and the reign of the Antichrist (2 Thess. 2:7-8; Luke 21:34-36; 1 Thess. 5:9). The Second Coming takes place after the tribulation (Rev. 19:11-21). The rapture may occur at any moment (Phil. 3:20-21; 1 Cor. 15:51). And the second coming cannot take place until the remaining prophecies are fulfilled."[14]

Charismatic theology defines the rapture as the first coming, and the return of Christ with His saints as the second coming.

A Primary Doctrine of the Church

It is interesting to note that when Paul founded the church at Thessalonica, one of the first doctrines he established was eschatology. Acts 17:1-2 records that Paul was in Thessalonica for only three weeks, during which there was mass conversion. What is remarkable is that in this short time Paul focused on the doctrine of the rapture and the second coming of Christ (2 Thess. 2:5).

In his first letter to the Thessalonians Paul had to correct them concerning those who had died in Christ. He goes to great lengths to tell them that those who have died will be reunited at the rapture with those who are alive.

> For this we say unto you by the word of the Lord, that we which are alive and remain unto the coming of the Lord shall not prevent [go before] them which are asleep. For the Lord himself shall descend from heaven with a shout, with the voice of the archangel, and with the trump of God: and the dead in Christ shall rise first: Then we which are alive and remain shall be caught up together with them in the clouds, to meet the Lord in the air: and so shall we ever be with the Lord (1 Thess. 4:15-17).

Bob Yandian, in his book *Resurrection — Our Victory Over Death*, speaks to this issue. "Paul emphasizes to the Thessalonians that their dead loved ones are not gone forever. He encourages them with the firm hope and assurance that one day the Lord Himself will return bringing with Him those who have gone on to glory."[15]

Victory Over the Grave

Fred Price agrees and takes the thought further by saying that only the body sleeps at death. Price says the body goes to the grave, but the spirit and soul of man go to be with the Lord. To be absent from the body means to be present with the Lord (2 Cor. 5:6-8).

Price, in his book *Concerning Them Which Are Asleep*, likens dying to wearing a suit and then hanging it up in your closet. While you are wearing the suit, the suit has a type of life to it; it takes on its own action and movement. But while it hangs on a hanger, it is lifeless. In the same way, Price says, "When you enter into that state of what we call death, all he (the spirit man) does is hang up the clothes (the physical body) in the closet (the grave or whatever place has become the temporary resting place)."[16]

Those who are "asleep" are only absent from their bodies; they are actually quite alive in the presence of the Lord. On that day when the trumpet sounds, and it will, those saints of old will come back and put on their transformed "earth suits."

Bob Yandian believes that it is at the rapture that total victory is won over the grave. At the rapture, he says, "The grave will lose its victory because it will no longer have the power either to threaten those believers who are still alive or to hold those who have already died." And in one of the most powerful statements about the rapture, Yandian says, "When our Lord arose from the dead, He left behind an empty tomb. When He comes again to redeem His church, He will leave behind millions of empty tombs!"[17]

> O death, where is thy sting? O grave, where is thy victory? (1 Cor. 15:55).

A Doctrine for New Converts

Paul chose to disciple his new converts in end-time theology (1 Thess. 4:15-17). Because of its practicality, the truth about the rapture and the second coming comforts those of us who have lost loved ones, and it helps us live holy lives so that we might be reunited with them on that day.

Paul continues this line of discipleship to the Thessalonian church in his second letter. Here we learn that he had clearly grounded the new converts in the doctrine of eschatology.

> Remember ye not, that, when I was yet with you, I told you these things? And now ye know what withholdeth that he might be revealed in his time (2 Thess. 2:5-6).

End-time teaching and preaching were part of the early church's fabric and makeup. In this letter Paul was addressing a problem which had arisen from his teaching on the end times. Some were causing trouble by saying that the rapture had already occurred. Paul opened 2 Thessalonians with these words, encouraging believers who were being persecuted:

> And to you who are troubled rest with us, when the Lord Jesus shall be revealed from heaven with his mighty angels, In flaming fire taking vengeance on them that know not God, and that obey not the gospel of our Lord Jesus Christ (2 Thess. 1:7-8).

Clearly, this text is speaking of the events which will surround the return of Christ at the end of the tribulation period, and it agrees with the rest of Scripture (Rev. 19:11-16; 2 Pet. 2:9-10).

There is a certain comfort in knowing that God is a just Judge, and that He, not we, will repay those who persecuted us unjustly (Rom. 12:19).

Next, Paul had to address the error that had crept into the church surrounding the doctrine of eschatology. Word had come to the church that the rapture had already taken place (2 Thess. 2:1-2). Paul addressed this in his first letter (1 Thess. 4:13-18). So the apostle writes this about the rapture in 2 Thessalonians 2:

> Now we beseech you, brethren, by the coming of our Lord Jesus Christ, and *by our gathering together unto him,* That ye be not soon shaken in mind, or be troubled, neither by spirit, nor by word, nor by letter as from us, as that the day of Christ is at hand.
>
> Let no man deceive you by any means: for that

day shall not come, except there come a falling
away first, and that man of sin be revealed, the
son of perdition; who opposeth and exalteth himself above all that is called God, or that is worshipped; so that he as God sitteth in the temple of
God, shewing himself that he is God (vv. 1-4,
italics added).

Dr. Roy Hicks says of the above text that the key
expression which distinguished between the two events of
the rapture and the second coming is our "gathering together" unto Christ. Hicks reminds us that at the return of
Christ, Jesus returns with the saints on white horses (Rev.
19:11-21). It is obvious that in order for the saints to return with Him, they already had to be gathered to Him at
some previous point. Hicks identifies this event as the
rapture.[18]

Then in 2 Thessalonians 2:2-3 Paul says that "the day of
Christ" cannot take place until the Antichrist is revealed.
The day of Christ is a day of judgment and wrath referred
to and prophesied about throughout the Old Testament.
The prophet Joel called this the "day of the Lord." It will
begin after the rapture of the church, and it will last for
seven years, concluding when Jesus returns to judge Antichrist and his armies. Thus, in correcting the error of the
church, Paul gives us a clear look at his doctrine of the two
events surrounding the last days, the rapture (our gathering
unto Him) and the second coming (the day of the Lord).

Is the Rapture an Escapist Theology?

Some have accused those who believe in the pretribulation rapture as being escapist. They say that those who
look for the rapture are not willing to suffer for Jesus.
However, charismatics are quick to note that the rapture
was never meant to be an "escape route."

Carman strongly exhorts the church to avoid escapist thinking. He warns us that from the "second century onward, there has been a continuous stream of end time predictions."[19] He cites several examples of people who have claimed to know the day or "season" of the Lord's return, including Edgar C. Wisenant, who published *88 Reasons Why the Rapture Will Be in 1988*.

> But of that day and hour knoweth no man, no, not the angels of heaven, but my Father only (Matt. 24:36).

"It is not as important to know when He is coming as it is that we live our lives in the light of His coming. But that doesn't mean we put on robes and go up the hill." Carman, a major charismatic voice using music as his medium, adds that we are to be found as "faithful stewards doing the Lord's bidding when He returns."[20]

> And the Lord said, Who then is that faithful and wise steward, whom his lord shall make ruler over his household, to give them their portion of meat in due season? Blessed is that servant, whom his lord when he cometh shall find so doing (Luke 12:42-43).

Carman concludes that we should fulfill our Master's expectations. Jesus will come and hold us to account for what we have done with the opportunities which He has entrusted to us. "Many Christians today think of the return of the Lord only in terms of escape, and the more they think about it, the more unfaithful they become."[21]

These hardly sound like the words of a person who is promoting escapist theology. I chose to quote Carman because he is not a theologian in the general sense of the word. I do not think he would classify himself as a teacher

— perhaps a preacher, but not a teacher — in the context of the ministry gifts of Ephesians 4:11-12. But Carman has embraced the theology of charismatic teachers. My contention is that we as charismatics are not looking for the rapture as an escape, but rather as a promise!

Oral Roberts, in his book *God's Timetable for the End Time!*, says that though we look for the appearing of Christ (Heb. 9:28), "This does not mean that God's faithful will never experience trials or bitter persecutions." Dr. Roberts says, "At this moment in various parts of the world, severe persecution, imprisonment, and even tortures are plaguing those who refuse to deny their Lord."[22]

While a graduate student at Oral Roberts University, I saw Dr. Roberts persecuted on more than one occasion. But he quoted the Bible, saying that while we face difficult things now, we will be delivered during the desperate period called the great tribulation. "The redeemed Bride of Christ will escape from the unspeakable terrors of the tribulation, by means of the rapture."[23]

> Because thou hast kept the word of my patience, I also will keep thee from the hour of temptation, which shall come upon all the world, to try them that dwell upon the earth. Behold, I come quickly: hold that fast which thou hast, that no man take thy crown (Rev. 3:10-11).

In the last chapter of his book *Occupy Until Christ Returns*, Dr. Roberts cites Luke 19:13, where Jesus tell us to occupy until He comes. Oral says that we are called to faithfulness which does not suggest "that we sell all that we possess and climb some hillside to await His coming." On the contrary, Oral concludes, "We have been entrusted with the opportunity to be Christians and soul winners at a time unparalleled in history."[24]

Roberts Liardon says, "When He returns, we are to be

found working and occupying. We ought to be busy obeying His directions, which may be building new churches, putting new ministries on television and radio, writing new books, or moving out in new evangelistic campaigns around the world."[25]

A close pastor friend of mine had Roberts Liardon in for a meeting recently. After the service I asked Roberts about his ministry in light of the last days. He shared with me that he is enjoying the days he is living in, and said, "The work of God is flourishing; we're enjoying possessing the land."

As charismatics, we are not fatalists, but we are fighters. Right up until the day that Jesus returns we are to be about the work of the kingdom of God and the winning of souls. Our eschatology should never discourage, but rather encourage the preaching of the gospel.

In the next chapter we will discuss the timing of the rapture in relationship to the tribulation period. Most charismatics believe that the rapture will take place before the tribulation period. There are, however, some who believe that the rapture will take place in the middle or at the end of the tribulation period. We will examine all three positions.

Practical Application

Many ministers overlook the value of teaching those who have lost loved ones about the rapture. This doctrinal area will comfort those who have had great losses. Actually, this is one of the reasons that the rapture became known as the "blessed hope" of the church. Hope always causes us to look forward to the future. Those who have lost loved ones can get stuck in the grief process. What better way to help them get on with their lives than by sharing the truth that one day in the future they will be reunited with those loved ones!

Second, if you are discipling new converts, do not overlook teaching them this doctrinal area. New converts, more than any others in the church, have the freshest contacts with the unsaved. They will share end-time truth with zeal if they are given an opportunity. However, be prepared, because it is my experience that when new converts begin to share about the end times with their friends and family, they often come back with many good questions about the rapture.

9

PRETRIBULATION RAPTURE

Spared From God's Wrath

As with all systematic theology, charismatic theology becomes more defined the further it is examined. We have seen thus far that charismatic writers are very unified in their end-time theology. So, as we look closer at the doctrine of the return of Christ, it is no surprise that the majority of charismatic teachers are pretribulationists. In other words, they believe that Jesus will return for the church before God judges the earth with wrath.

Marilyn Hickey says, "God does not want His children to

89

experience these horrors. In a tender act of protection, much like a father pulling his child from the dangers of deep water, Jesus gathers us in His arms. This gathering together to Christ is the Rapture." Marilyn says, "The tribulation begins after the Rapture."[1]

For further proof of the pretribulational position, Dr. Roy Hicks turns to the many examples of deliverance within Scripture. He writes, "If God saved Noah, and his family from destruction, saved Lot from the fiery wrath on Sodom, and sent Joseph into Egypt to prepare a place to save Jacob from famine, and by prophecy told the Jews when to flee Jerusalem from the wrath of the invading Roman emperor Titus so that they escaped, then it is absolutely unthinkable that a born-again Church will have to face the wrath of God or the Anti-Christ, who would do unspeakable things to the Body of Christ, His Bride."[2]

Oral Roberts in his commentary agrees, writing that when the Antichrist arises, his nature of wrath will be revealed. He will cause the world to receive his mark, and those who do not receive it will be martyred by the devil during the great tribulation. "And so the Lord is not going to let his people go through that tribulation period."[3] Therefore we must convert as many people as possible now, before the rapture occurs, because after the rapture, the only way to heaven will be through martyrdom. For further biblical proof I would like to examine 1 Thessalonians 5:9:

> For God hath not appointed us to wrath, but to obtain salvation by our Lord Jesus Christ.

The wider context of this verse can be seen in 1 Thessalonians 4:17 – 5:9. In the fourth chapter, Paul dealt with the rapture of the church and those saints who had died in Christ. At the beginning of chapter 5 he writes, "But of the times and the seasons, brethren, ye have no need that I write unto you" (v. 1).

The church of Thessalonica had no need for Paul to write them about that for they already knew that the rapture would occur like a thief in the night. Paul is writing them concerning end-time events, and he is comforting them. When he writes to them that they are not appointed to wrath, but instead to deliverance, the apostle is bringing great assurance to the church about their future.

Other Positions in Charismatic Circles

In the next three chapters we will further explore the pretribulation position because it is the most widely accepted. But do charismatics take other positions on the timing of the rapture during the tribulation period? The answer is yes.

Morris Cerullo appears to be a midtribulationist; Pat Robertson is a posttribulationist; and Jack Hayford seems to be between both of these. It is interesting that no one in charismatic circles outside the pretribulation camp seems to be vocal about his position. As a matter of fact, in researching this project I found that the views of these men I mentioned are obscure, and they stay away from catch phrases which would commit them to these positions.

I had to call Living Way Ministries to find published material on Jack Hayford's position, only to discover that Dr. Hayford has not published on this subject. When I asked if he would, the response I received was, "Probably not because he does not want to cause division in the body of Christ."

Some may find that alarming, but I find that dignified. Charismatics agree on a lot, and one of our strengths is to stay focused on these issues and on soul-winning. Once again, we see the pragmatic side of charismatic theology.

Practical Application

In seminary, before finals or major presentations, you can hear the graduate theology students asking one another if they are ready, and many jokingly respond, "No, I am praying for the rapture." In reality none of us would want to stand before God and tell Him why we are not ready. But a certain hope lies in the idea that no matter how bad things get, one day very soon things are going to get a whole lot better.

Paul wrote the persecuted churches of Thessalonica and Rome, using this doctrine to encourage them. We will all experience trials, temptations and persecutions. As Christians we are not to cry and complain. We walk by faith, not by sight.

As a pastor, there have been times when I had to walk before my congregation in faith, while circumstances said something else. In extreme moments like this in my ministry, all I had to hold on to was the blessed hope that it had to get better. Do you know what? It always did get better. In those times all I had to hold on to was the Word of God, but that was all that I needed. I was able to stand with victory, and that was what the people needed to see!

10

DANIEL: ONE WEEK UNTIL MIDNIGHT

A Literal Seven Years

Charismatic theology widely accepts a literal seven-year tribulation period, but where does this idea come from? The two primary biblical sources for the seven-year tribulation period are the books of Daniel and Revelation. In this chapter we will examine Daniel's seventy weeks, and in the next chapter we will walk through the chronology of the seven years of tribulation as it is found in the book of Revelation.

Jesus' End-Time Instruction

Jesus tells us in Matthew 24 that if we want to define the tribulation period, we must go to the book of Daniel.

> When ye therefore shall see the abomination of desolation, *spoken of by Daniel the prophet,* stand in the holy place, (whoso readeth, let him understand:)...For then shall be great tribulation, such as was not since the beginning of the world to this time, no, nor ever shall be (vv. 15,21, italics added).

Remember that the disciples did not have the New Testament to understand end-time theology. Jesus instructs them to study the book of Daniel and his reference to the "abomination of desolation" (Dan. 9:24-27).

I did an intensive verse-by-verse Bible study of the entire book of Daniel with a group of adults in our church. We discovered that while Daniel was in captivity under both the Babylonian and Medo-Persian empires, he pressed into end-time theology. In each successive chapter of the book of Daniel, prophecy unfolds in a greater and more detailed way.

At first Daniel had only a glimpse of the end times, and he was not satisfied. He pressed into the spiritual realm until he received more truth. For example, in Daniel 2 he interprets King Nebuchadnezzar's dream, which is a brief overview of the four remaining kingdoms which would rise and fall before God sets up His kingdom. But by the seventh chapter his vision of these kingdoms is greatly expanded. Now we see Daniel actually enter the vision and interact with an angel about its meaning. By the ninth chapter Daniel is fasting, speaking in depth to angels and having great details given to him about the last days and the rule of the Antichrist.

It is in the ninth chapter that Gabriel comes to Daniel and

uncovers the end-time truth about the Antichrist and the setting up of his image in the temple. The "abomination of desolation" which Jesus refers to is found in Daniel 9:24-27. It is also in this text that we discover the length of the tribulation period.

Daniel's Seventy Years

Dr. Cho, in his work *Daniel: Insight on the Life and Dreams of the Prophet from Babylon,* observes that Daniel heard from the angel Gabriel about a prophecy that Jeremiah had given. Jeremiah had prophesied that the Jewish nation would be in captivity for seventy years (Jer. 25:11).[1] Daniel says he came to understand the words of Jeremiah.

> In the first year of Darius the son of Ahasuerus, of the seed of the Medes, which was made king over the realm of the Chaldeans; in the first year of his reign I Daniel understood by books the number of the years, whereof the word of the Lord came to Jeremiah the prophet, that he would accomplish seventy years in the desolations of Jerusalem (Dan. 9:1-2).

Jeremiah's prophecy that Israel would go into captivity was fulfilled in 605 B.C. when Nebuchadnezzar and the Babylonian armies raided Jerusalem. Daniel was taken captive and led into Babylon.

In 538 B.C. (sixty-seven years later) the Medo-Persian empire overthrew the Babylonians, and Darius, the Mede, was given reign over the region of Babylon. At that time, Daniel began to intercede on behalf of Israel because he recognized that their seventy years of captivity were almost over. With the transitions of government, Daniel saw the fulfillment of Jeremiah's prophecy that Israel would come out of captivity in seventy years.

Carlton Pearson points out that during Darius's reign, God raised up Esther, Nehemiah and Ezra to bring the Jews out of captivity and back to Israel. I believe that Nehemiah and Ezra found favor with the king to rebuild the walls of Jerusalem because of the prayers of Daniel (Dan. 9:3-4; Neh. 2:7-8; Ezra 1:1-3). It was no coincidence that the king of Persia first commanded that Jerusalem be rebuilt in 538 B.C. — the very time that Daniel began to pray!

End-Time Revival Is Here!

Pearson makes practical application of Daniel 9:1-2. He says that believers today are in bondage just as Israel was in bondage. But he believes that the church's time of bondage is over. "It's time for the chains to fall off. It's time for revival, renewal, restoration — time for us to be conquerors."[3]

I couldn't agree more. I believe we are experiencing only the beginning of the great end-time revival prophesied in Scripture (Acts 2:16-21; James 5:7-8). As we approach the end of the age, the church is going to be prepared for the return of Christ. In order for that to happen the church must first be free in every area. There will be an end-time revival like this world has never seen before.

Kim Clement says that what is happening now is more than a simple revival that will come and go. "The Lord has shown me again and again that what is on the horizon is far greater than a breath of fresh air or a revival." Clement continues, "It is more than a visitation from above, in which the Lord comes, and then He leaves. We are going to experience a 'habitation' of the Holy One. It will be permanent. He will come and reside!"[4]

Daniel Stands on the Word

Remember, Daniel was only a teenager when he was taken into captivity, but he had held on to Jeremiah's prophecy that Israel's bondage would only last seventy years. When he was in his eighties, he began to fast and pray, repenting for the sins which caused Israel to go into captivity (Dan. 9:1-20). He was anticipating Israel's release because the seventy years were almost over. In response to Daniel's prayer Gabriel comes and reveals not only when Israel would return to Jerusalem, but also the rest of Israel's history in great detail.

> Seventy weeks are determined upon thy people and upon thy holy city, to finish the transgression, and to make an end of sins, and to make reconciliation for iniquity, and to bring in everlasting righteousness, and to seal up the vision and prophecy, and to anoint the most Holy (Dan. 9:24).

In Daniel 9:24-27, charismatics see a unique time scale. Oral Roberts calls this the seventy weeks of Daniel "which will follow the dispensation of the Gospel Age."[5]

Dr. Cho gives the classical interpretation of this text, explaining that the Hebrew word translated *weeks* means *sevens*. Therefore, the word of the Lord to Daniel is that seventy weeks, or "sevens," (70 x 7 = 490 years) are determined for Israel and the city of Jerusalem. At the end of this time "everlasting righteousness" will be completely established, which, of course, has not yet happened.

> Know therefore and understand, that from the going forth of the commandment to restore and to build Jerusalem unto the Messiah the Prince shall be seven weeks, and threescore weeks: the street shall be built again, and the wall, even in troublous times. And after threescore weeks shall Messiah be cut off, but not for himself (Dan. 9:25-26a).

483 Years Until Messiah

Next, Gabriel established the specifics of the prophecy. He said that from the time that the ruling king released Israel to rebuild Jerusalem until the time of the Messiah would be seven plus sixty-two "sevens," or 483 years.

At the same time that Daniel is in the Spirit having this vision, Nehemiah and Ezra are being spoken to by God. The books of Nehemiah and Ezra record these events. In Nehemiah 2 we see King Artaxerxes releasing Nehemiah to rebuild the walls of Jerusalem.

Historians tell us that from the time Nehemiah was sent to Jerusalem to the triumphant entry of Christ into Jerusalem was exactly 483 years, or sixty-nine "sevens."[6] Marilyn Hickey agrees. "Jesus arrived 483 years after the temple was rebuilt. When the Jews rejected Him, the Jewish Age was suspended and the Church Age began. The Jewish Age resumes again when the church is raptured, but one week still remains on the clock."[7]

At this point in the prophecy Daniel learns of the crucifixion of Christ. He came to His own, but they did not receive Him. Israel rejected their Savior.

> And after threescore weeks shall Messiah be cut off, but not for himself (Dan. 9:26a).

This prophecy is given 483 years before the fact. Daniel is writing prophecy which would not be fulfilled until the time of Christ. God's Word is extremely prophetic. Lester Sumrall says that this is proof that God is God. Many years before these events took place, "God through his servants reveals the empires' likeness, their strength, their rise and fall, and the one that would succeed them."[8] But even with all this the Jewish people did not recognize Jesus as the one about whom Daniel prophesied.

Death of Christ and the Rise of Antichrist

Jesus the Messiah was to be cut off — not for Himself, but for the entire world (Dan. 9:26a; 2 Cor. 5:16-21). Satan blinded the religious leadership of the Jewish nation, and they rejected and crucified the Messiah (Luke 23:13-23).

Then Daniel sees far beyond Christ's crucifixion to the day that the Antichrist would reign and fulfill the words of Jesus about the "abomination of desolation."

> And the people of the prince that shall come shall destroy the city and the sanctuary; and the end thereof shall be with a flood, and unto the end of the war desolations are determined (Dan. 9:26b).

Two very important points emerge from this text. First, an angel is speaking to Daniel, which gives us a clue to angelic roles among mankind. Second, the focus of the prophecy has to do with the temple and Daniel's people, Israel.

Now, remember that in Matthew 24 the temple is the focus of discussion which caused Christ to address the end times and instruct the disciples to consult the book of Daniel. Jesus also said the temple would be destroyed. In A.D. 70 the temple was destroyed, but it must yet be rebuilt. Then the Antichrist will set himself up in it as God.

Hal Lindsey, a regular guest and host on Trinity Broadcasting Network, says that a prince will arise who will "make a firm covenant with the Jewish people. This prince must arise from the Roman Empire." Lindsey quotes the apostle Paul concerning the "abomination of desolation" and says, "Paul speaks of this person as one who opposes and exalts himself above every so-called god or object of worship, so that he takes his seat in the temple displaying himself as being God (2 Thess. 2:4, NAS)."[9]

In his discourse in Matthew 24, Jesus told us to go to the book of Daniel. He wanted those who study the Bible to understand the end of the age and the great deception Satan would bring through a false christ.

Antichrist and the End-Time Temple

First, the Antichrist will make a seven-year covenant (one week is equal to seven years) with the Jewish people. I believe the covenant will consist of a contract for the Antichrist to rebuild the temple on the old temple site (Dan. 9:27; 2 Thess. 2:4). Once the temple is rebuilt, the Jews can reinstate the sacrificial system. Then, in the middle of the "week," or after three-and-a-half years, the Antichrist will break the covenant.

> And he shall confirm the covenant with many for one week: and in the midst of the week he shall cause the sacrifice and the oblation to cease, and for the overspreading of abominations he shall make it desolate, even until the consummation, and that determined shall be poured upon the desolate (Dan. 9:27).

Presently, the Dome of the Rock, the second most important Moslem mosque, is on the very site where the temple must be built. In order for the Antichrist to make a covenant involving the rebuilding of the temple, there must be a treaty between Israel and the Arab nations surrounding her. This will be no small task. However, we see the first signs of such a treaty on the horizon.

Oral Roberts says that when Jesus told us to go back and study about the "abomination of desolation" in Daniel, he was saying that the Antichrist will stand in the temple and declare himself to be God. Roberts calls this "the most dreaded time in history."[10]

It is also important to note that the temple does not need to be rebuilt before Jesus returns. With modern technology the temple could easily be built in the first three-and-a-half years of the Antichrist's reign. By the midpoint of the tribulation the temple must be built in order for this text to be fulfilled. The "abomination of desolation" then is clearly at the middle of the tribulation period, when the Antichrist proclaims himself to be God in the temple of God (2 Thess. 2:4; Rev. 13:56).

Daniel does not reveal the details of the second three-and-a-half years of the tribulation period. In Daniel 10 and 11 he is given details about spiritual warfare and the rise and fall of future empires. Then in the twelfth chapter Daniel is told about "Jacob's time of trouble," but he is told to shut up the revelation of the vision (Dan. 12:4) because it is for the end of time. The time of trouble which Daniel saw was the second three-and-a-half years of the tribulation period.

As charismatics we believe that we are in the end times, and we believe that God is revealing those things which were shut up to Daniel. In the next chapter we shall see the details of these events as they unfold in the book of Revelation.

Practical Application

We can learn some very practical truths from Daniel about how to move deeper into spiritual things. Daniel saw prophecy fulfilled in his lifetime. He interpreted the signs of the times and stood on the Word of God as it was given by Jeremiah. We, too, are living in the midst of global changes, and we must hold tighter to the Word of God than any other generation has needed to. Believers in our day and time are called to do great exploits. To do these, we must draw closer in our relationship with God just as Daniel did.

Hebrews tells us that angels are ministering spirits sent to minister to the heirs of salvation. In the last days the Word of God tells us that angelic activity will increase (Matt. 13:39,49; 16:27; 25:31-32; Acts 1:11; Rev. 14:15). We must become familiar and comfortable with the idea that angels not only exist, but that they may be sent with assignments to minister to us as they did to Daniel.

Fasting also should be a part of the believer's life in the last days. Jesus said that while the Bridegroom was with the bride there would be no need for fasting. But when the Bridegroom is taken away, then the bride would need to fast (Matt. 9:15).

11

JOHN'S REVELATION
OF CHRIST

A Literal and Chronological Account

The book of Daniel ended with an angel instructing Daniel to go his way because "the words are closed up and sealed till the time of the end" (Dan. 12:9). The book of Revelation ends with an angel instructing John, "*Seal not* the sayings of the prophecy of this book: for the time is at hand" (Rev. 22:10, italics added). God withholds truth until mankind is ready for it. John was told that it was time to reveal the truths about the end of this age. He opens the book of Revelation with these words:

103

> The Revelation of Jesus Christ, which God gave unto him, to show unto his servants things which *must shortly come to pass*; and he sent and signified it by his angel unto his servant John (Rev. 1:1, italics added).

John was told that these end-time events were going to happen "shortly." Then, because of the lateness of the hour, John encourages all believers to study these prophecies, adding:

> Blessed is he that readeth, and they that hear the words of this prophecy, and keep those things which are written therein: for the time is at hand (Rev. 1:3).

As with all the promises of God, this promise is two-fold. First, there is a blessing for those who will study this prophecy. Second, there is a condition to the blessing, that we must "keep," or do, the things which have been prophesied. As you have read through this book, you have seen much that you need to do. As you step out in these areas you should expect a blessing because God has promised to bless those who study this prophecy.

Three Major Divisions to the Revelation

Most charismatics take the Word of God literally. We believe that God said what He said, and meant what He said. Therefore, the majority of charismatics take the book of Revelation literally — and chronologically.

Three major chronological divisions are found in the book of Revelation. John reveals these three divisions in Revelation 1:19. Jesus commands John to write in three tenses: past, present and future:

> Write the things which thou hast seen, and the

things which are, and the things which shall be hereafter.

These are the three divisions of the book of Revelation:

1. "The things which thou hast seen." These are those things which John saw in Revelation 1.

2. "The things which are." Jesus tells John about the seven churches in Revelation 2 and 3.

3. "The things which shall be hereafter." This includes the literal seven-year tribulation period found in Revelation 4 through 19, the millennium and the great White Throne judgment in 20, and the new heavens and the new earth in 20 and 21.

As charismatics, we hold to common truths found in the book of Revelation. In this chapter we will identify those truths found in each of these divisions.

Division One: "The Things Which Thou Hast Seen"

The entire first chapter makes up the first division, the things John had already seen. In this chapter John prophesied about the second coming of Jesus, and he saw a supernatural appearance of Christ in His glorified form.

First, John saw the second coming of Jesus. In Revelation 1:7 he wrote, "He cometh with clouds; and every eye shall see him." John was clearly not referring to the rapture. Dr. Cho says, "At the rapture of the church Jesus does not reveal Himself to the world but rather comes only to gather the believers as they rise to meet Him in the clouds (1 Thess. 4:17)."[1] The event of the rapture takes place "in a moment, in the twinkling of an eye" (1 Cor. 15:52), and only we who are looking for the Lord will see Him. But the event which John witnessed is the second coming, seven years after the rapture (Rev. 1:7).

Second, John saw Jesus in all of His glory. His head and hair were white, His eyes were like flames, and His feet were like brass. In His right hand were seven stars, which represent seven angels, and He was standing in the middle of seven candlesticks, which represent the seven churches.

The purpose of the first division is to set the stage. John is about to be called up to heaven in the great rapture of the church. John will interact with angels and even participate in the next two divisions of the revelation.

Division Two: "The Things Which Are"

Next, John is looking at Jesus holding seven stars, which are the seven angels, standing in the midst of the seven candlesticks, which are the seven churches. The second division to the book of Revelation is the seven messages to the seven churches, "the things which are."

Most scholars believe that these seven angelic messages represent divisions of the church age. These seven messages are prophecies given to the church applying to different periods of time over the past two thousand years. Marilyn Hickey agrees and gives us the following historic view:

1. The church of Ephesus represents the church of the apostolic age, A.D. 96

2. The church of Smyrna represents the church of persecution, beginning about A.D. 97

3. The church of Pergamos represents the church of imperial favor, beginning about A.D. 312

4. The church of Thyatira represents the church of papacy, beginning about A.D. 450

5. The church of Sardis represents the church of the Reformation, beginning about A.D. 1517

6. The church of Philadelphia represents the church of the latter day outpouring, from the present through the end of the age.

7. The church of Laodicea represents the lukewarm church, from the present through the end of the age.[2]

The last two messages, those to the churches of Philadelphia and Laodicea, are prophecies to our generation. John saw that in the last generation two churches would co-exist. One would be radical, full of the power of God and doing great exploits (Dan. 11:32); the other would be lukewarm and lethargic, and would compromise with the world (Rev. 3:14-22).

Just before the turn of this century there began a great outpouring of the Holy Spirit on the church. This is represented by the church of Philadelphia to whom the gifts of the Spirit were restored. There came a fresh understanding of the need for the baptism in the Holy Spirit. Knowledge of the end-time doctrine was also restored during this time period.

Jesus gave this powerful promise for those who are prepared and waiting for His return:

> Because thou hast kept the word of my patience, I also will keep thee from the hour of temptation, which shall come upon all the world, to try them that dwell upon the earth (Rev. 3:10).

Jesus will rapture the church of Philadelphia out of the earth before the "hour of temptation" known as the tribulation period. At the same time He warns the church of Laodicea that they must come out of their lukewarm state or go through the tribulation.

> And unto the angel of the church of the Laodiceans write...I know thy works, that thou art neither cold nor hot: I would thou wert cold or hot. So then because thou art lukewarm, and neither cold nor hot, I will spue thee out of my mouth.
>
> Behold, I stand at the door, and knock: if any man hear my voice, and open the door, I will come in to him, and will sup with him, and he with me (Rev. 3:14-15,20).

The last words of this division, "the things which are," tell us that Jesus stands at the door and knocks. Get this picture into your spirit. Jesus is at the door of heaven, and He is pounding, saying, "My return is near. Prepare!" In the very next verse John sees the rapture, which is the beginning of the third and last division the one that makes up the majority of the book of Revelation.

Division Three: "The Things Which Shall Be Hereafter"

> After this I looked, and, behold, a door was opened in heaven: and the first voice which I heard was as it were of a trumpet talking with me; which said, Come up hither, and I will shew thee things which must be hereafter (Rev. 4:1).

There is only one event that I know of that includes a door in heaven opening, a trumpet sounding and a voice calling, "Come up hither!" This is clearly the rapture of the church as Paul records in his epistles (1 Cor. 15:51-52; 1 Thess. 4:16-17). This third division consists of a literal seven-year tribulation period, the return of Christ with the saints, the millennial reign of Christ, the great White Throne judgment, the new heavens and the new earth.

There are two major periods in the literal seven-year tribulation period. Each are three-and-a-half years in length.

108

These periods are referred as "times, time and a half" (see Dan. 12:7 and Rev. 12:14).

It should be clarified that several charismatic teachers, including Dr. Yonggi Cho, Finis Dake, Dr. Gordon Lindsay and Marilyn Hickey, believe that the first half of the seven-year tribulation period will be one of peace compared to the second half. Dr. Cho in his commentary on the book of Revelation divides the tribulation period into two parts. He sees the first three-and-a-half years discussed in chapters 6 through 10, and the second three-and-a-half years in 11 through 19.[3] Marilyn Hickey has a slightly different interpretation. She believes that 4 through 11 are the entire tribulation period as viewed from an earthly view, while 12 through 16 are the same events from a heavenly view.[4]

The First Half of the Tribulation

During the first three-and-a-half years, Antichrist shall be revealed, the temple shall be rebuilt, and God will begin to pour out His wrath on the earth. During this period of time, great numbers of people will come to the Lord (Rev. 7:9-10). Those of the "church of Laodicea" will see the error of their ways and repent. In addition, 144,000 Jews will be converted at this time (Rev. 7:4-8). I believe the Jews and the church of Laodicea are two separate groups saved during the first half of the tribulation.

Revelation 4 opens with the rapture. John is taken in the Spirit to the throne room of God. The remainder of the chapter is an experience in heavenly worship (vv. 3-11).

God the Father is holding a book sealed with seven seals (5:1). No one is found worthy to open the book. John then sees Jesus appear in a type of royal procession (vv. 2-14). The Lamb, Jesus, is the only one who is worthy to open the book (6:1). He takes the book, breaks the first seal, and the tribulation period begins. As each seal is opened, the following events take place (vv. 1-17):

1. The first seal breaks open to reveal a white horse. Antichrist is released from restraint to go and conquer.

2. A red horse comes out of the second seal, as a bloody war ensues.

3. The black horse of the third seal represents the famine which followed the end of the war.

4. The fourth seal reveals the pale horse of death which follows the famine.

5. As the fifth seal is broken, the people converted to Christ are martyred.

6. A great earthquake follows the breaking of the sixth seal

7. The seventh seal reveals the seven trumpets which announce the impending judgments of God.

By the opening of the sixth seal, the earth is well into experiencing the beginning of the wrath of God. Kings, generals and the great men of the earth cry out:

> Fall on us, and hide us from the face of him that sitteth on the throne, and from the wrath of the Lamb: For the great day of his wrath is come; and who shall be able to stand? (Rev. 6:16-17).

Revelation 7 opens with the conversion of 144,000 Jews. These Jewish people are sealed with protection from Antichrist, and they become evangelists during the remainder of the tribulation period.

Some charismatic teachers see in verse 9 a second rapture following the sealing of these evangelists. "After this I beheld, and lo, a great multitude, which no man could number, of all nations" (7:9a). According to Marilyn Hickey, these

144,000 Jewish evangelists will bring in a great harvest during the tribulation period. "This rapture is an act of mercy on the gentiles who accept Christ during this great torture, despair and trouble." Marilyn calls this the "Great Harvest Rapture."[5]

The seventh seal which Jesus opened consisted of the seven trumpets (8:1), with the sounding of the first of these occurring in verse 7. Trumpets have always played a significant role in the history of Israel. Joseph Good, a TBN personality and Jewish scholar, shows us various uses of the trumpet in his book *Rosh Hashanah and the Messianic Kingdom to Come*. Quoting the Old Testament and other Jewish works, he says that the trumpet used in Israel was called a "shofar or a ram's horn." It was "used to announce the beginning of festivals, to muster troops, to warn of danger, to assemble the people in the midst of battles, and for coronations."[6]

These seven trumpets warn of the impending judgments of God. Until the first trumpet is sounded, God has left man to his own destruction. Now, in the sounding of these seven trumpets, we see God begin to pour out His wrath on the earth and its inhabitants. Chapters 8 and 9 list the results of six of the seven trumpets:

1. The first trumpet. One-third of the earth's vegetation burns up.

2. The second trumpet. One-third of the sea, the creatures and the ships in it are destroyed.

3. The third trumpet. One-third of the fresh water is destroyed.

4. The fourth trumpet. One-third of the sun, moon and stars are destroyed.

5. The fifth trumpet. Demonic scorpions are loosed.

111

6. The sixth trumpet. One-third of mankind is killed by three plagues.

7. The seventh trumpet is not sounded until Revelation 11:15. It is followed by great voices in heaven proclaiming:

> The kingdoms of this world are become the kingdoms of our Lord, and of his Christ; and he shall reign for ever and ever (11:15).

At this point in the book of Revelation (11:1-12), God's heart is revealed more than in any other place in the Word. We are at the three-and-a-half year mark, and God sends another evangelistic campaign to the earth. God's heart is after souls; He does not desire that any should perish, but that all should come to repentance (see 2 Peter 3:9 in its context). His wrath is only another sign and a call to repentance.

God's desire that none perish is shown when midway through the revelation an angel comes to John and tells him to preach and prophecy (see Rev. 10). Then chapter 11 opens with God sending two witnesses to testify about Jesus. These two witnesses cannot be harmed. They will convert a great number of people into the kingdom of God. Then, in Revelation 14 we see an angel flying around preaching a message of repentance (vv. 6-7).

The Second Half of the Tribulation

Jesus uses the expression "great tribulation" to describe the coming catastrophic period.

> For then shall be *great tribulation,* such as was not since the beginning of the world to this time, no, nor ever shall be. And except those days should be shortened, there should no flesh be

saved: but for the elect's sake those days shall be shortened (Matt. 24:21-22, italics added).

The word in the Greek for "great" is the word *mega*, and the Greek word for "tribulation" is *thlipsis*. There can be only one interpretation to this Greek construction: "an intense period of wrath." Jesus tells His disciples that no generation has experienced what this last generation will see. The elect which Christ is referring to here are the converts during the tribulation period. For their sake this period will be cut short. In reality, three-and-a-half years is a very short period, less than the length of a Presidential term.

Dr. John Walvoord, an accepted theologian amongst charismatics, believes the above text (Matt. 24:21-22) is a reference to the "last three-and-a-half years, leading up to the Second Coming. In that time, there will be specific signs that will unmistakably identify the period as the time of the Great Tribulation."[7]

Some charismatics believe in a midtribulation rapture of the church. Proponents of a midtribulation return of Christ for His church believe that wrath will not be poured out on the earth until the church is caught up. Some writers who believe that Christ's second coming will be at the end of the tribulation period still maintain that God has the ability to deliver the believer in the midst of wrath just as He did the Israelites in the land of Goshen when He poured out the plagues upon Egypt. One point of agreement among charismatics is that God will not punish His children with wrath.

We do not see references to God's wrath again until the end of Revelation 15. God's perfect number is seven, and the His last acts consist of pouring out the seven vials of wrath on the earth (16:1-21). John sees seven angels, each standing with a vial of wrath ready to pour out on the earth. Here is a summary of each angel's activity:

1. The first angel pours out a vial that causes sores on those with the mark of the beast.

2. The second angel pours out a vial that kills everything in the sea.

3. The third angel pours out a vial that destroys the fresh water supply.

4. The fourth angel pours out a vial upon the sun, causing it to scorch mankind.

5. The fifth angel pours out a vial that causes darkness and pain on the Antichrist's kingdom.

6. The sixth angel pours out a vial that dries up the Euphrates river, making a way for the battle of Armageddon.

7. The seventh angel pours out a vial that releases the great earthquake upon the earth.

The remainder of the book of Revelation reveals the fall of the great harlot (the religious system of the Antichrist) and the city of Babylon (Rev. 17 – 18). This is followed by a great cry from heaven, and Jesus leaps on His horse.

> And I saw heaven opened, and behold a white horse; and he that sat upon him was called Faithful and True, and in righteousness he doth judge and make war. His eyes were as a flame of fire, and on his head were many crowns; and he had a name written, that no man knew, but he himself. And he was clothed with a vesture dipped in blood: and his name is called The Word of God.
>
> And the armies which were in heaven followed him upon white horses, clothed in fine linen, white and clean. And out of his mouth goeth a sharp sword, that with it he should smite the nations: and

he shall rule them with a rod of iron: and he tread-
eth the winepress of the fierceness and wrath of
Almighty God.

And he hath on his vesture and on his thigh a
name written, KING OF KINGS, AND LORD OF
LORDS (Rev. 19:11-16).

The kings of the East assemble themselves for battle at
Armageddon in an attempt to overthrow the Antichrist
(Rev. 16:16). The kings of the East then join the Antichrist
to fight Christ and His army, but even with all of their high-
tech weaponry, they never even get a shot off. Jesus, the
Word, opens His mouth, and it is V-Day! John's revelation
is a book of victory. The tribulation period ends, and the
millennium begins.

Practical Application

I am convinced that God is evangelistic. Even during the
tribulation period we see God reaching out to those who
remain on the earth. If anything is holding back the return
of Christ, it is God's desire to see more people saved (Rom.
9:22-23). The church's lack of evangelism may be holding
up His return. We must do whatever is necessary to win the
world around us to Christ before the tribulation begins.

Many of those who are saved during the tribulation period
will make it to heaven only by being martyred. It will not be
a pleasant time on earth. We must use these truths to convert
the lost to Christ now, before it is too late for them.

Like David, we must possess a heart after God. May the
"church of Philadelphia," the bride of Christ, begin to pray
like John Knox prayed for England, "Give me England or
give me death!"

12

THE MILLENNIUM — NOW OR LATER?

Satan Is Still Loose

S ome say that we are living in the millennium now. Yet the Word teaches that at the beginning of the millennium, Satan will be bound and cast into the pit.

> And he [the angel] laid hold on the dragon, that old serpent, which is the Devil, and Satan, and bound him a thousand years (Rev. 20:2).

It does not take a whole lot of common sense to look at society and history and figure out that Satan is not, nor has

116

he ever been, bound. Quite the contrary, with all the increase of lawlessness, satanic worship and new age philosophy, psychic phone lines and gang violence, one can logically deduce that we are not experiencing the millennium of Christ's rule with a rod of iron keeping evil in check.

So why the theological conflict that has caused some to err by believing that we are in the millennium? In the next chapter we will discuss what the millennium will be like, but first I want to show that charismatics do not believe that we are currently in the millennial reign, which some have referred to as the New World Order. I believe the reason for this error is a paradox we find in Scripture.

The Kingdom Already, But Not Yet

There is an expression in theological circles which goes like this: the kingdom of God is here, but not fully. In other words, "already, but not yet."[1] The concept is biblical because Jesus said the kingdom of God has come unto you (Matt. 12:28), yet He also told us to pray for the kingdom to come (Matt. 6:10).

Dr. Larry Lea, in his book *The Weapons of Your Warfare*, gives us a great illustration to explain this concept. He uses the World War II analogy of what happened on June 6, 1944, otherwise known as D-Day. On that day the allied forces won a decisive battle, and the war turned around completely. But Lea points out that it took another year for Germany to surrender on that great day known as V-Day.

Jesus Christ won the decisive battle for us at the cross, and mopping up is all that is left. "Satan was defeated. But until Jesus comes again in victory to establish His kingdom officially and force Satan to surrender all authority to Him, the church is engaged in the final throes of the war."[2]

Jack Hayford, in his article "A Present and Future Kingdom," agrees with the "already, but not yet" concept.

He writes, "The kingdom is being realized *presently*, in partial and personal ways, as it is spread *through* the Earth by the Holy Spirit's power in the church." Hayford believes the church is in a battle headed for victory as the kingdom of God expands in the earth. Of the final victory, Hayford adds these words, "The kingdom will be realized *finally* in consummate and conclusive ways only at the return of Jesus Christ and by His reign *over* all the earth."[3]

Pastor Tommy Reid, in his book *Kingdom Now But Not Yet*, agrees that the "emphasis on the presentness of the Kingdom, without recognition of the future aspect of the Kingdom, is dangerous. The church argues today over whether the Kingdom is present or future. Emphatically, it is both. There has been no golden age in the past, and there will be no golden age till He comes again."[4]

One of the best writers in this area is Pat Robertson. In his book *The Secret Kingdom*, Robertson says that a secret kingdom is already operating on earth, the kingdom of God. According to Robertson, the kingdom of God is moving forward in the midst of a society that is growing cold, and it will continue to move forward until one catastrophic day when the "invisible Kingdom of God becomes visible." That day is the return of Christ and the beginning of the millennium.

Robertson calls this the "transition period, between the earth as it has been, and the ultimate plan of God, in which evil and opposition to the Lord will be finally removed and paradise established." The length of the new period will be a literal thousand years, and Robertson says, "hence the name millennium. In it Christ will reign and there will be peace."[5]

A Word About Dispensations

A word that is thrown around a lot is *dispensations*. Simply defined, the word means "periods." Bob Yandian, whom we have already introduced as a powerful expositor in the charismatic movement, defines the idea of dispensations. In his work *Salt and Light*, Yandian addresses the various dispensations in the Word of God. Dispensations simply put are periods of time or ways that God has dealt differently with man throughout history.

Yandian says that from the cross to this present day we have been in the dispensation of grace or the dispensation of the church age. "The church age will go all the way until the Rapture, and after the Rapture, the earth will go into a seven-year tribulation." He continues, "After the tribulation will come the dispensation which is the Millennium."[6]

It is important not to confuse the use of dispensations with the theological system called Dispensationalism. Charismatics believe in a literal dispensation called the millennium, which is a far cry from dispensationalists who believe that signs and wonders stopped with the apostles. When charismatics use the word *dispensation*, they are simply referring to a period of time.

When Will We See World Peace?

Many scholars believe that the Sermon on the Mount will be enforced during Jesus' millennial reign. Pat Robertson holds to this traditional thinking and believes that Jesus gave us this message as a pattern of "new laws" or "laws of the Kingdom." We feel the tension of living in the kingdom of God now under these laws, yet still living within the world system. Robertson says that these laws will prevail in the millennium and the people of God will rule with Jesus according to these precepts. "Food, water, and energy will be ample. No longer will trillions of dollars be spent on weaponry."[7] In conclusion, Robertson says that true peace will not be achieved until the millennium.

Isaiah no doubt had this in mind when he wrote:

> And it shall come to pass in the last days, that the mountain of the Lord's house shall be established [Jesus reigning in Jerusalem] in the top of the mountains, and shall be exalted above the hills; and all nations shall flow unto it...*for out of Zion shall go forth the law*, and the word of the Lord from Jerusalem. And he shall judge among the nations, and shall rebuke many people: and they shall beat their swords into plowshares, and their spears into pruning hooks: *nation shall not lift up sword against nation, neither shall they learn war* any more (Is. 2:2-4, italics added).

Bob Yandian writes in *One Nation Under God* that organizations which try to bring world peace in this dispensation are "deceived because they cannot bring complete lasting peace." Yandian points out that this passage of Scripture is a reference to when "Jesus will set up His millennial Kingdom on this earth." He says, "Satan is the author of war; so long as Satan is on the earth, there will be wars."[8]

Paul also warns us that during these last days we should beware of those who call for world peace:

> For yourselves know perfectly that the day of the Lord so cometh as a thief in the night. For when they shall say, Peace and safety; then sudden destruction cometh upon them, as travail upon a woman with child; and they shall not escape (1 Thess. 5:2-3).

Over the past several years we have seen false prophecies come and go, along with the tendency to set dates and times about a reign of peace. Sound doctrine dictates that these events will not take place until Jesus sets up His reign in the earth. Until then there will be wars and rumors of wars (Matt. 24:6).

The New World Order

Pat Robertson used the phrase "the new world order" long before President Bush brought it up during the Gulf War crisis in 1991. In 1982, he wrote that Jesus wants us to learn how to operate in the principles of the kingdom in this life "so [we] will be ready for the new world order that appears to be rushing toward us."[9]

Then, almost ten years later, Robertson declared: "God's new world order is coming much nearer than we believed. God's work is right on schedule. The company of the sons of God is almost complete — perhaps this very decade may finish the task." He concludes by saying: "Finally, let us remember that the triumph of God's world order is certain. This is the decade of opportunity for the church of Jesus Christ."[10]

These words of opportunity should ring in our hearts. I believe with everything in me that what we do here in this life will directly affect our lives in the millennium. Jesus said that those who were faithful with little would be made rulers over much. One day we will live and reign with Christ for a thousand years. We will be priests of God and of Christ, and we will reign with Him (Rev. 1:6; 20:3-4). Our questions should be, Who will we reign over, and what will it be like? In the next chapter we will look at that reign in great detail.

Practical Application

We are not yet in the millennium, but as we see the day approaching, we must press into our prospective areas of vocation. We are called to be salt and light (Matt. 5:13-16). Salt preserves and light provides direction. We must not retreat from society; we must advance. As the end of time draws closer, the body of Christ is to be actively involved in every arena — economically, socially and politically. Oral

Roberts would say, "We are to go into every man's world."

Let me share a final word about technology. I have heard it said that technology is of the devil. Personally, I have a hard time believing that the devil is in control of releasing knowledge.

Several years ago I ran into an old schoolmate who went into the communications field, working for one of the largest communications companies in the world. In our conversation he related that he felt as though he was preparing the way for the mark of the beast. After some time of reflection on his conversation, I came to the conclusion that he was not a part of fulfilling the devil's plan, but God's. Antichrist's reign and his usage of technology will be very short-lived.

Knowledge is increasing at a rapid rate. I believe that God is releasing knowledge to advance His plan, not the devil's. This knowledge will be put to good use during the millennium. As we see that day drawing nigh we should expect advances in society, and, better yet, we should be a part of them!

13

THE MILLENNIAL REIGN OF CHRIST

The Believer's Reward and Rule

So, what will it be like to have the devil bound for a thousand years? What will take place during the millennium? What will we do for a thousand years? Who will we rule and reign over, and how? Scripture has a lot more to say about the millennium than most of us realize.

> And he [the angel] laid hold on the dragon, that old serpent, which is the Devil, and Satan, and bound him a thousand years...and [they] which had not worshipped the beast, neither his image,

neither had received his mark upon their fore-
heads, or in their hands; and they lived and
reigned with Christ a thousand years...they shall
be priests of God and of Christ, and shall reign
with him a thousand years (Rev. 20:2,4,6).

A Literal Thousand-Year Reign

Once again, as we turn to this doctrinal area of charismatic theology, we find it extremely unified. The vast
majority of us believe in a literal thousand-year reign of
Jesus from the holy city, Jerusalem. Even those who may
have been midtribulationist or posttribulationist in reference to the rapture still believe in a literal millennial reign
of Christ.

Prophecy Fulfilled

Prophecy will prevail, and the kingdom of Jesus will be
established. Daniel gives us a summary statement about the
end of this world's kingdoms and the rise of the last eternal
kingdom.

Thou sawest till that a *stone* was cut out without
hands, which smote the image upon his feet that
were of iron and clay, and break them to pieces.
Then was the iron, the clay, the brass, the silver,
and the gold, broken to pieces together, and
became like the chaff of the summer threshingfloors; and the wind carried them away, that no
place was found for them: and *the stone* that
smote the image became a great mountain, and
filled the whole earth (Dan. 2:34-35, italics added).

This text is the result of the prophet Daniel having his
back against the wall. King Nebuchadnezzar had a dream

which troubled him greatly. He called for his wise men to interpret the dream or be killed. But God gave Daniel the interpretation of the dream, and in doing so, He provided us with an overview of all the remaining kingdoms that would exist on the earth.

Lester Sumrall identifies the stone in Nebuchadnezzar's dream as Jesus. He says that Jesus "is the Rock of Ages. He is the Smiting *Stone*. He is the Cornerstone of all civilization." Sumrall then interprets the phrase "a stone cut without hands" to mean that Jesus was "born of a virgin," thus becoming the King of kings without the assistance of any man.[1]

Dr. Stanley Horton and Dr. William Menzies agree that this text is a reference to the end of the age, the battle of all battles and the setting up of the millennial kingdom of Christ. In their combined work, *Bible Doctrines: A Pentecostal Perspective*, they tie Daniel's interpretation to the triumphant event of the return of Christ with His saints found in Revelation 19:

> And I saw heaven opened, and behold a white horse; and he that sat upon him...doth judge and make war...and His name is called The Word of God.
> And the armies which were in heaven followed him...And out of his mouth goeth a sharp sword, that with it he should smite the nations: and he shall rule them with a rod of iron (vv. 11,13-15).

Horton and Menzies write, "This is the fulfillment of Daniel 2:34-35, where the 'stone' destroys the kingdoms of this world and then becomes a kingdom that fills the earth."[2]

Sumrall notes further that the empires of men "shall become like chaff of the summer threshingfloors. The wind will carry them away. No place will be found for them." He says that Jesus "shall rule over this earth for a thousand years; there will be no memories of these despotic empires which sought to rule man and the world."[3]

The Earth's Population Will Be Replenished

Because of the tribulation's devastation to over three-fourths of the world's population and its resources, the earth will need to be repopulated. In Revelation 20 we discover that at the end of the thousand years, the earth will be filled with a large population (v. 8). So who will populate the earth?

We who have returned with Christ will be in our glorified bodies (1 Cor. 15:50-54). Scripture teaches us that when we see Him we will be like He is (1 John 3:2; Phil. 3:20-21). We will have bodies in the likeness of Christ, neither marrying nor being given in marriage.

Finis Dake says that those who are converted during the tribulation period and at the return of Christ shall remain in their natural bodies and propagate (Rev. 20:8). I believe also that there are those who will not be converted, but will have not received the mark of the beast. They will go into the millennium alive in their mortal bodies.

The Devil Bound for a Thousand Years

During the millennium Satan will be bound; wars will cease, but not by the hand of man. Pat Robertson says, "Everything that is offensive will be removed from the kingdom of God, not by men or the church or military might."[4] And we who are believers "eagerly look forward to the establishment of God's new world order when evil, hatred, sickness, poverty, and war are taken from the earth."[5]

In order for this to take place the devil must be bound. God has designed a holding place especially for the devil. I look forward to the day when all believers will look at the devil and say, "How did he cause the nations of the world trouble?" (Is. 14:16). What a sight that will be to watch the devil being bound and chained! Gordon Lindsay says: "Just prior to the Millennium, [the devil] will be cast down into this dark pit, no doubt to lash about in fury, but impotent to do anything. He will brood and plan new schemes of deception for the time that he will be released for that little season at the close of the millennium (Rev. 20:7-9)."[6]

It is important that the believer understands that at the end of the millennium, he will have a glorified body (1 Cor. 15:50-54; 1 John 3:2; Phil. 3:20-21) and will not be tempted by the devil. Those who enter the millennium from the tribulation period will multiply and be in number like the sand of the sea, many of whom will be a part of the final rebellion (Rev. 20:7-10).

The Believer's Reward and Rule

John's Revelation on Patmos begins and ends speaking of the millennial reign of Christ and His saints:

> And from Jesus Christ, who is the faithful witness, and the first begotten of the dead, and the *prince of the kings* of the earth. Unto him that loved us, and washed us from our sins in his own blood, and hath made us *kings and priests* unto God and his Father; to him be glory and dominion for ever and ever. Amen (Rev. 1:5-6, italics added).

> *They shall be priests* of God and of Christ, and shall reign with him a thousand years (Rev. 20:6b, italics added).

An interesting phrase is used throughout the body of Christ, especially in charismatic circles: "Jesus is King of

127

kings and Lord of lords!" We have written songs about this, and many charismatic ministers use the phrase.

Have you ever wondered who those "kings and lords" are? The Greek word for "king" is the word *basileus,* which means "royalty, or one who rules a realm or a kingdom." Jesus is referring to a rule and a reign which is governed by priestly dictates.

The book of Revelation records Jesus coming with the armies of heaven to fight the Antichrist and his armies. Jesus is on His white horse and has a banner across His chest and the name "King of kings and Lord of lords" written on his thigh (Rev. 19:16). Those kings and lords to which He is referring are the ones who are riding side by side with Him. They are you and me, the faithful saints who have obeyed His Word in deed in this life!

Jesus has already made us a kingdom of priests (Rev. 1:5-6; 20:4-6). We as charismatics believe that we have begun to rule and reign with Christ in the here and now. Those who have been called out of darkness are not only living in the light, but we have also become a "royal priesthood, an holy nation" (1 Pet. 2:9). The kingdom of God has come, yet not in all of its fullness. What we do in the here and now will determine what we will do in the millennium.

The Millennial Parable of the Talents

In the parable of the talents we find out how Jesus will determine who will hold which positions in the millennium. Luke records for us the context of this parable:

> He [Jesus] added and spake a parable, because he was nigh to Jerusalem, and because *they thought that the kingdom of God should immediately appear* (Luke 19:11, italics added).

One of the reasons Jesus taught this parable was to show

people about the kingdom of God. The disciples, in line with Jewish thinking, believed that the kingdom would manifest quickly, by force; it would exist in a completed form; and it would deliver them from all their enemies. Jesus wanted to correct their thinking.

The location Jesus chose to tell the parable of the talents is very important. He was approaching Jerusalem, and the disciples knew the Old Testament promises of the physical reign of God from Jerusalem.

> And many people shall go and say, Come ye, and let us go up to the mountain of the Lord...and he will teach us of his ways...for out of Zion shall go forth the law, and the word of the Lord *from Jerusalem. And he shall judge among the nations*...and they shall beat their swords into plowshares, and their spears into pruninghooks: nation shall not lift up sword against nation neither shall they learn war anymore (Is. 2:3-4, italics added).

The Jews were looking for the Messiah, and many wanted Jesus to take His rightful place as a reigning king. It was in this heated atmosphere that Jesus gave the parable of the talents.

Jesus opens with a king who went far away from home to receive another kingdom, then returned. This king had left certain servants in charge of his kingdom, and he had given to each of them a portion of the finances to accomplish their set tasks.

Upon his return, the king found that two of the servants had been faithful to accomplish the tasks he left for them, while one had not. What is important in this parable is how the king judged his servants righteously. The worthless slave was stripped of all he had because of his lack of faithfulness to do what he knew he should do. The book of

129

Proverbs contains these same kingdom ethics — that the lazy person or the sluggard not only chooses a path of poverty, but also ultimately one of total destruction (Prov. 6:6-15).

On the other hand, what the king said to the faithful servants speaks to us about the rewards we shall receive in the millennium. He praised them, then he gave them authority in his kingdom.

> And he said unto him, Well, thou good servant: because thou hast been faithful in a very little, have thou authority over ten cities...And he said likewise to him [the second servant], Be thou also over five cities (Luke 19:17,19).

Many verses in Proverbs confirm these kingdom ethics, saying that the diligent shall rule (Prov. 10:4; 12:24-27; 13:4; 21:5; 22:29).

What is important in life is finding God's will and doing it. Our society has promoted the idea of living for the moment, but God has called to us to plan to live for an eternity! How we do what God tells us to do right now will determine how we live in the millennium.

The Disciples Reign in the Region of Israel

On a different occasion Peter asked Jesus what he and the disciples would receive as a reward for having forsaken all to follow Him. Jesus told him that they would rule over the tribes of Israel.

> And Jesus said unto them, Verily I say unto you, that ye which have followed me, in the regeneration when the Son of man shall sit in the throne of his glory, ye also shall sit upon twelve thrones, judging the twelve tribes of Israel (Matt. 19:28).

Remember that each tribe was allotted land throughout Israel. According to their faithfulness the disciples will rule with Christ in the regions of Israel. How the disciples lived in obedience to the Word will determine how they will reign in the millennium.

I believe that the parable of the talents is speaking of the reward system based on our faithfulness in this life that God has set up for the millennium. I also believe that during the millennium Jesus will rule and reign from Jerusalem, and that He will appoint a government under Him who will rule with Him around the world (Is. 2:3-4; Ps. 2:9; Rev. 12:5).

We Shall Reign With Christ!

While I was a student at Oral Roberts University I heard Dr. Roberts jokingly say more than once that in the millennium he would be returning to Tulsa to run the city. While this was said jokingly, it might not be far from the truth. There is no question that our works will be judged and we will be rewarded according to what we have done (1 Cor. 3:14-15; 2 Cor. 5:10). Perhaps Oral Roberts will be rewarded in the millennium with a key leadership position over that city.

Some Christians have the mistaken idea that during the millennium they will sit around and drink milk and eat honey. But if I read my Bible correctly we will not be sitting around doing nothing. We will be building, leading and reigning with Christ.

Jesus will establish His physical throne in the city of Jerusalem (Is. 2:2-4). We will take our assignments and orders from Him. A tremendous amount of work will need to be done immediately as a result of the wrath of God which was poured out on the earth during the tribulation period. We will reign over those who did not receive the mark of the beast and enter the millennium out of the tribulation period. They will procreate and have children as numerous as "the sand of the sea" (Rev. 20:8).

For the first time in the history of mankind there will be a genuine theocratic government — a government God-centered and God-designed. This is the government which the prophets described, including Daniel:

> And the kingdom and dominion, and the greatness of the kingdom under the whole heaven, shall be given to the people of the saints of the most High, whose kingdom is an everlasting kingdom, and all dominions shall serve and obey him (Dan. 7:27).

Isaiah also prophesied about God's government:

> For unto us a child is born, unto us a son is given: *and the government shall be upon his shoulder:* and his name shall be called Wonderful, Counsellor, The mighty God, The everlasting Father, The Prince of Peace (Is. 9:6, italics added).

> And there shall come forth a rod out of the stem of Jesse, and a Branch shall grow out of his roots...But with righteousness shall he judge the poor, and reprove with equity for the meek of the earth: and he shall smite the earth with the rod of his mouth (Is. 11:1,4).

The Psalmist records a similar prophecy, words from the Father to Jesus:

> Ask of me, and I shall give Thee the heathen for thine inheritance, and the uttermost parts of the earth for thy possession. Thou shalt break them with a rod of iron; thou shalt dash them in pieces like a potter's vessel (Ps. 2:8-9).

Jesus says that the overcomer will rule with Him. He gives us a direct quotation from the Psalms:

And he that overcometh, and keepeth my works unto the end, to him will *I give power over the nations: And he shall rule them with a rod of iron;* as the vessels of a potter shall they be broken to shivers: even as I received of my Father (Rev. 2:26-27, italics added).

This tells us of the type of government which shall be in operation during the millennium. Jesus' government shall operate from the law and with the rod of iron (Rev. 12:5; 19:15).

In his book *A Thousand Years of Peace*, Gordon Lindsay wrote an entire chapter on "The Millennial Government." He said the first thing that Jesus will do is destroy and disarm the nations (Is. 2:4). "The material used in the armaments, the guns, the tanks, and the war planes will all be junked; and the metals will be melted down for peaceful uses." Dr. Lindsay believed that much of the energies of mankind will be directed to bringing an end to things such as poverty.[7]

The theocratic reign of Christ will create an earth with real equality. Micah 4:4 says that every man will rest under his own vine and under his fig tree and that there shall be no fear.

The Earth's Thousand Years of Rest

Prophecy indicates that during the millennium the earth will find rest. Genesis records of the earth being cursed (Gen. 3:17-19). Sin has taken its devastating toll on the earth, and the earth is crying out for its restoration (Rom. 8:19-22).

Before man sinned there was utopia in the garden. Oral

133

Roberts believes that earth will be restored to what it was like before the fall. In his commentary on the New Testament, Oral concludes, "This is what God originally had in mind when he placed Adam and Eve in the Garden." God created the garden as a place of utopia for the purpose of being able to fellowship with man. Oral says, "I am looking forward to that day when we will once again have full communion and fellowship with God our Creator."[8]

A final note about what the millennium will be like. Isaiah 11 tells us:

> The cow will feed with the bear, their young will lie down together, and the lion will eat straw like the ox. The infant will play near the hole of the cobra, and the young child put his hand into the viper's nest (Is. 11:7-8, NIV).

On one hand, the world will be very much like it is now; but it will be nothing like it is now in regard to ethics and morality. The glory of the Lord will fill the earth. His kingdom will truly be led by the Spirit of God. No wonder all of creation groans for the final redemption of man and the revealing of the sons of God (Rom. 8:19-22). In a very real sense, creation will find its rest.

In the next two chapters we will discuss the judgment of the righteous and the unrighteous. How we live now will, without question, affect how we will be judged and how we will live in the next move of God.

Practical Application

At a glance the doctrine of the millennium may not look very practical. After all, it is way off in the future, isn't it? Not many of us in the body of Christ think about the millennium.

But consider that our lives here consist of maybe seventy to a hundred years. The millennium will last a thousand years! With all of the talk in the body of Christ about time management, goals and leadership training, you would think we would make some really long-term goals!

When we realize that our lives in the millennium will be an extension of how we are living and obeying in the present, we will be more serious about knowing and doing the will of God here and now. Also, keep in mind that our lifestyle in the millennium will be better because we will not be limited to the confines of these earthly tents. We will be able to travel as Jesus traveled in His glorified body — through walls, and transported from spot to spot (Luke 24:31,36,51; John 20:19,26; Acts 1:9). These are practical truths that motivate us to think before we act on our own plans. We must find the purpose and plan of God for our lives and be as Paul: obedient to the heavenly vision (Acts 26:19).

14

A LITERAL HEAVEN AND HELL

Eternal Destiny for All Mankind

Charismatics are unified in their belief in a literal heaven and a literal hell. So much is written in theological circles and by cults that tries to make heaven and hell less than what God's Word says they are. Heaven and hell are not places of limbo or sleep. Scripture clearly points to a literal place called heaven and a literal place called hell. Hell is a place of eternal separation from God, and heaven is a place of eternal reward (Matt. 25:31-46).

One thing we all have in common is that one day, unless the rapture occurs first, we will face the greatest enemy of mankind — death itself. This subject of life after death is one of the strongest areas of charismatic theology. Because charismatics believe in a literal heaven and a literal hell, we have a strong focus on evangelizing souls.

Rod Parsley, a young firebrand preaching machine who has been discipled by Dr. Lester Sumrall, calls the body of Christ back to this doctrinal truth. In his book *Holiness: Living Leaven Free*, he says the church once again needs to believe in a literal heaven and hell. Parsley gives us his thinking on the Bible being taken literally by saying, "It is time the church returned to Bible basics, and believed that God said what He meant and meant what He said!"[1]

Heaven: Our Future Home and God's Eternal Home

Creflo Dollar, pastor of a ten-thousand-member congregation in Atlanta, Georgia, writes that he is convinced "that very few believers have grasped the reality of heaven. If they had, they wouldn't act the way they do." He says that it may be obvious, "but the first thing you need to know about heaven is that God dwells there."[2]

God's Word tells us that He created heaven as His dwelling place (Is. 66:1; 1 Kin. 8:27; Jon. 1:9). He created the angelic armies of heaven who dwell with Him (Gen. 2:1). It is from heaven that God looks down from His throne and hears our prayers, and makes the sun to shine and the rain to fall on the just and the unjust (Deut. 26:15; 1 Kin. 22:19; Matt. 5:45, 6:1). God watches and opens His windows of heaven and pours out blessings to those who obey in the giving of tithes and offerings (Mal. 3:10; Matt. 6:1).

We are seated in heavenly places, and we should be comfortable with the idea of living there. Heaven is an incredible place where God planned our born-again experience to flow from. We have an inheritance that does not fade away and is reserved for us there (1 Pet. 1:4; Phil. 3:20).

Jesus came from heaven and returned there after His resurrection to become our High Priest at the right hand of the Father (Mark 16:19; Heb. 8:1-2). In the same manner that Jesus left for heaven — "in the clouds of heaven" — He will return to deliver us from the coming wrath of the tribulation period (Matt. 24:30; Mark 14:62; Acts 1:11; 1 Thess. 1:10).

Acts 3:21 tells us that Jesus will remain in heaven until the restitution of all things. When the gospel is preached in all the earth, and the fullness of gentiles has come in, then Jesus will be sent from heaven. We are waiting eagerly for His soon return so He can take us back with Him. Rod Parsley adds, "We need a church anxious to go to that heavenly city that rises 1500 miles high, with walls made of jasper, and gates made of a single pearl 300 feet high"[3] (see Rev. 21).

Heaven – Now or Later?

A major part of what we believe about heaven affects how we live in the here and now. As we have said, we believe that once we are saved we are positionally made to sit in heavenly places, and we can begin to possess eternal things now. Charismatics do not believe that you must wait until you get to heaven to receive eternal rewards.

Yet we are not saying that we possess all things right now, nor that we have attained some permanent state of perfection. What charismatics are saying is that we should not be limited to a thinking which says, Now that I am saved all that I have to do is to hold on until I die, then things will be all right. On the contrary, we are saying that we can possess the sweet by-and-by in the here and now!

Peter asked Jesus what he would receive for forsaking all and following Him. Jesus replied to Peter and all those who would follow him that they would receive "an hundredfold now in this time, houses, and brethren, and sisters, and mothers, and children, and lands, with persecutions; and in the world to come eternal life" (Mark 10:28-30).

Myles Munroe addresses possessing eternity here and now in his book *Understanding Your Potential.* He says that God designed us to live forever, and many people do not reach their potential because they do not understand that. He asks the question, "What are we are going to do in heaven?" He concludes that God has a lot in mind for us to do, and he adds that we will need all of eternity to accomplish it. Myles quotes 1 Corinthians 2:9:

> But as it is written, Eye hath not seen, nor ear heard, neither have entered into the heart of man, the things which God hath prepared for them that love him.

In a great quotation, Myles says, "Your true potential requires eternal life to be realized and maximized."[4] This is clear-cut charismatic thinking. Eternity begins now, and we should strive for the gold concerning God's will for our lives.

Rev. Kenneth E. Hagin says the same thing in his book *Zoe: The God Kind of Life.* Rev. Hagin defines the Greek word *zoe* as "eternal life, or God's life." He says that when we are saved, we receive the nature of God, and we become a new creation. He cites John 5:24:

> Verily, verily, I say unto you, He that heareth my word, and believeth on him that sent me, hath everlasting life, and shall not come into condemnation; but is passed from death unto life.

Then Rev. Hagin says: "You've got life now. You're not going to get it when you get to heaven. Thank God, you have it now." Later in the book, Rev. Hagin quotes Ephesians 2:2-6, which says that we are now seated in heavenly places with Christ Jesus. Then Rev. Hagin asks: "Have we identified with Christ in what He did? So when are we to reign as kings? During the Millennium? In 'the sweet by and by'?" "No," he says, "It begins in this life!"[5]

This may sound simplistic, but it is profound theologically. We are saying that we do not have to wait until heaven to appropriate many of the promises of God. We can and should operate in eternal things now. What we are learning and experiencing now is an extension of heaven, and it is God's will. That is why Jesus told us to pray on a daily basis that "Thy kingdom come. Thy will be done" (Matt. 6:10).

How we have learned to operate in the Word here is only an extension of how heaven operates. Hebrews 11:3 tells us "the worlds were framed by the word of God." God in heaven operates by His Word. Our rewards and millennial duties will be a reflection of how well we obeyed the things we knew to do here (2 Cor. 5:10; Luke 19:17). Many Word of Faith teachers believe that there will be ongoing training in the Word during the millennium for those who did not learn how to operate in the Word in this dispensation.

> Not as though I had already attained, either were already perfect: but I follow after, if that I may apprehend that for which also I am apprehended of Christ Jesus. Brethren, I count not myself to have apprehended: but this one thing I do, forgetting those things which are behind, and reaching forth unto those things which are before, I press toward the mark for the prize of the high calling of God in Christ Jesus (Phil. 3:12-14).

Joyce Meyer, a woman with a powerful ministry to broken people, says that Paul often used the metaphor likening the Christian to a runner running a race (1 Cor. 9:24-27). She says that we need to hold on to Jesus, who

140

has purchased salvation for us. As we trust in the Lord He will bring us to the finish line.

Then Joyce, in true charismatic form, says that salvation is more than a home in heaven. "Your eternal salvation began the day you were born again, and it will never end."[6]

Hell: A Place of Eternal Separation

We can make some strong comparisons between heaven and hell. For example, there will be no memory of sin in heaven, but in hell there will be the constant tormenting reminder of sin which separated mankind from its Creator. In heaven there will be no memory of lost loved ones, yet in hell there is a cry to see one's relatives (Luke 16:23-28).

T. D. Jakes makes reference to the second death and eternal damnation (Rev. 21:8) in his book *Can You Stand to Be Blessed?* Jakes says that the second death is called that not because we come to the end of consciousness, but because when we die in our sins we are separated from God.

Bishop Jakes says: "Without debating your concepts of hell, I am sure you would agree that eternity without God is a type of hell itself. That is what the book of Revelation calls the second death. It is eternal separation from the presence of God. It is the final step of sin. Sin is separation of relationship with God, but the second death is separation from the presence of God!"[7]

Rod Parsley writes about eternal separation citing the teaching of Jesus about Lazarus and the rich man (Luke 16:19-31).

> The rich man also died, and was buried; and being in hell he lift up his eyes, being in torments, and seeth Abraham afar off, and Lazarus in his bosom. And he cried and said, Father Abraham, have mercy on me, and send Lazarus, that he may

dip the tip of his finger in water, and cool my tongue; for I am tormented in this flame. But Abraham said, Son, remember that thou in thy lifetime receivedst thy good things, and likewise Lazarus evil things: but now he is comforted, and thou art tormented (Luke 16:22-25).

Benny Hinn notes that the rich man was taken to hell, and he was conscious of torment. "Hell is a place of torment and fire and those who go there are very aware of the torment."[8]

Creflo Dollar says that we learn several things about hell from the parable of the rich man and Lazarus. "First, we find that it's a place of torment. Hell is not going to be a place where you sit around and socialize. It's a place of agony and utter despair. The rich man's torment was so intense, he believed a single drop of water might bring him some relief." Second, Creflo Dollar says, "If you end up in hell, one of the first things you'll start thinking about are your friends and family."[9]

A Biblical Concept of Hell

As charismatics we believe in a literal hell that is a holding place of torment until the day of judgment when hell shall give up its dead and be thrown into the lake of fire (Rev. 20:13-14).

Benny Hinn, in his book *War in the Heavenlies*, identifies five different "underworlds": Tartarus, the prison of angels (1 Pet. 3:19); Paradise, a holding place for the Old Testament saints (Luke 16:19-23); Sheol, or hell, the abode of the wicked dead (Ps. 55:15); Abyss (Luke 8:31); and Gehenna, the eternal lake of fire (Rev. 20:14).[10]

Hell is the product of God's anger at the devil's rebellion (Matt. 25:41; Deut. 32:22). Isaiah tells us that hell is waiting for the devil: "Hell from beneath is moved for thee to meet thee at thy coming" (Is. 14:9). In Revelation we discover the devil will be bound in "the bottomless pit" for a thousand years (Rev. 20:1-2). I believe the bottomless pit referenced in Revelation is a separate area within hell. Some of those who fell with the devil have already been bound in hell.

> God spared not the angels that sinned, but cast them down to hell, and delivered them into chains of darkness, to be reserved unto judgment (2 Pet. 2:4).

There is much debate about where hell is, but the Word tells us that it is in the center of the earth. Hell is deep (Job 11:8; Prov. 15:24), it is never full, and it has the capacity to enlarge itself (Prov. 27:20; Is. 5:14; Hab. 2:5).

Who is sent to hell, and what will they experience? First, it should be noted that Jesus gave His strongest warnings about hell to the religious community of his day, those who were religious outwardly, but whose hearts were not right (Matt. 23:15,33). Jesus told the religious leaders that out of the abundance of the heart the mouth speaks (Matt. 12:34). James also addresses the religious leaders, "The tongue is a fire, a world of iniquity: so is the tongue among our members, that it defileth the whole body, and setteth on fire the course of nature; and it is set on fire of hell" (James 3:6).

The wicked, even though they were strong in the earth, are sent to hell (Ps. 9:17; 55:15; Ezek. 31:16; 32:21). Some have even made a covenant with hell (Is. 28:15). All who go to hell will experience a fire which cannot be quenched (Matt. 5:22,29). Jesus tells us that those who go to hell receive a body which cannot perish, and they experience much torment, sorrow and pain (2 Sam. 22:6; Ps. 18:5; 116:3). He also says that not only do their bodies go to hell, but also their souls (Matt. 10:28).

Entire communities can be in danger of being brought down to hell:

> And thou, Capernaum, which art exalted unto hea-
> ven, shalt be brought down to hell (Matt. 11:23a).

Only one thing will prevail against hell, and that is the
church of Jesus Christ (Matt. 16:18). That means you and
me as believers, and we must take seriously the responsibility of delivering those who are headed there.

Visions of Heaven, Hell and the Second Coming

As charismatics we believe in Joel's prophecy that the
young will have visions and the old will have dreams (Joel
2:28). Some people have supernaturally been moved by
visions of heaven, hell and by words about the second
coming. Roberts Liardon, for example, has written a book
I Saw Heaven, about the vision of heaven he had when
he was twelve years old. Dr. Richard Eby was clinically
dead and had a vision of heaven and hell. He records his
experience in *Caught Up Into Paradise*. Morris Cerullo
had a vision of two footprints, and when he looked into
them he saw the tormented souls of hell.[11]

Dwight Thompson, in his book *Devil, You Can't Have
My Family*, tells of an experience his brother had in the
middle of the night. Dwight, the son of a preacher, was
backslidden and running from God. His brother was awak-
ened in the middle of the night, and the Lord allowed him
to see a vision of Dwight dying in a car accident. Then he
saw Dwight being taken to hell in flames and torment.
Dwight's brother ran from his room to Dwight's room and
began to intercede for him. God told him that he would
save him and bring him back if he would stand in the
gap.[12] Dwight's brother never broke covenant with God.
Dwight writes, "My brother made a commitment to God
and he would not let my soul go to hell. He stood in the
gap for me for ninety days. That's why I'm preaching the
Gospel now."[13]

Oral Roberts says that one of the driving forces behind his ministry was a word that God gave to him while he was preparing a sermon in his motel room one night. He heard the words, "It is later than you think." Next, those words blazed before his eyes: It is later than you think. Oral says that those words have stayed with him down through the years as he has worked for God.[14]

Maria Woodworth-Etter records several dreams and visions she had in her diary. As a woman who was a healing evangelist, she was ahead of her time. She was a spiritual pioneer, especially in the area of dreams and visions. In one case, she was ministering at the altars to one last person when she had an open vision of heaven. An open vision, as I understand it, is a vision viewed with spiritual eyes, but as real as something viewed with physical eyes. She writes, "I saw the steps leading across to the Pearly Gates of Heaven...at the top of the Steps were the Pearly Gates, where the Heavenly Hosts waited to welcome the Pilgrims of Earth."[15]

Creflo Dollar said this is only logical. "The first thing you're going to see when you die are angels coming to escort you to heaven. It makes sense when you think about it. When you're entering a realm you've never seen before, you need some guidance."[16]

Maria Woodworth-Etter also had a vision on her bed. In her diary she writes, "The Lord showed me the Vision is concerning the Soon Coming of Christ." Was this vision important to her ministry? Yes! She writes: "In that Vision the Lord gave me a special call for this work, and to give the Household of Faith their Meat in due season; to give the Last Call to the Gentile sinners, the Last Call to the Marriage Supper of the Lamb, for His wife is about ready to enter the marriage relationship, and the door will be closed never to be opened again; and to get those who have been called to be established, to be faithful and true, that they be anointed with the Holy Ghost and with power, and sealed with the proper knowledge of His coming, and their great work during the millennial reign of a thousand years, when the saints shall judge the world and angels, when all the families of the earth shall be blessed."[17]

Even in moments when she was near death, Mrs. Woodworth-Etter held onto this vision. "I have been very near death several times, but the memory of the wonderful vision has inspired me to new life." Writing in 1916 she concluded, "The time is very short."[18]

These are just a few examples of how charismatics have been moved by visions and dreams. But what do they all have in common? From each of these experiences great sacrifices have been made and ministries have been birthed to reach a world dying and going to hell. As charismatics we believe God does not want anyone to go to hell. Visions and dreams have not brought us away from the will of God, but closer to His very nature and heartbeat. No wonder Dr. Cho says that dreams and visions are the language of the Holy Spirit.

> The Lord is...longsuffering to us-ward, not willing that any should perish, but that all should come to repentance (2 Pet. 3:9).

Practical Application

A production titled "Heaven's Gates and Hell's Flames" is making a tremendous impact in churches across America. The thrust of this production is very simple.

It contains ten scenes in which people die of various causes, such as car accidents, suicides, overdoses, plane crashes and elevators catching on fire. After every scene those who died either go to heaven or hell. If their names are not written in the Lamb's Book of Life, they go to hell.

If their names are in the Book of Life, they go to heaven in a triumphant procession.

The production is simple, yet profound. Audiences who come to see "Heaven's Gates and Hell's Flames" are confronted with what they know they will encounter one day. When the altar call is given large percentages of the audiences make decisions for Christ.

I want to encourage every person reading this book to rethink the area of preaching and teaching on heaven and hell. Our church put on a similar production, and in two nights we saw over two hundred people come to Christ. We must do everything we can to deliver souls out of hell.

Richard Roberts shares part of the testimony of his conversion in his book, *How You Can Touch Heaven With Your Faith*. He says that many well-intentioned people tried to persuade him to open up his heart to Christ. "But it wasn't until I came to the startling revelation that there was something at the end of this life — a hell to shun and a Heaven to gain — that I suddenly decided I wanted God in my life."[19]

Remember that you too were bound for hell. Never forget where you have come from and where others are headed. If those people around you do not get saved, they will spend an eternity not just in hell, but in a place worse than that. They will burn in the lake of fire (Rev. 20:14-15).

15

THE FINAL JUDGMENT

A Time of Celebration for Believers

We are living in a day and time when much teaching focuses on grace. However, it would be error to avoid balancing the teaching of grace with teaching of judgment and wrath. Remember that it was Jesus whose death brought us into grace and who also taught us that God is a God of judgment and wrath. Jesus gave the parable of the final judgment:

> Again, the kingdom of heaven is like unto a net, that was cast into the sea, and gathered of every

148

kind: Which, when it was full, they drew to shore, and sat down, and gathered the good into vessels, but cast the bad away. So shall it be at the end of the world: the angels shall come forth, and sever the wicked from among the just, and shall cast them into the furnace of fire: there shall be wailing and gnashing of teeth (Matt. 13:47-50).

Jesus said on another occasion, "Every idle word that men shall speak, they shall give account thereof in the day of judgment" (Matt. 12:36). And on that day "There shall be weeping and gnashing of teeth, when ye shall see Abraham, and Isaac, and Jacob, and all the prophets, in the kingdom of God, and you yourselves thrust out" (Luke 13:28).

Four Judgments

It is appointed unto men once to die, but after this the judgment (Heb. 9:27).

Judgment is inevitable, yet not all judgment will be sorrowful. The judgment of the believer will actually be a time of celebration. In this chapter we will examine four different judgments: the judgment of believers, the judgment of Israel, the judgment of unbelievers and the judgment of angels.

The Judgment Seat of Christ

The judgment seat of Christ is for believers. Some charismatics say this event occurs during the tribulation period, just following the rapture, at the marriage supper of the Lamb. Others believe this event will occur at the beginning of the millennium.

> For we must all appear before the judgment seat of Christ; that every one may receive the things done in his body, according to that he hath done, whether it be good or bad (2 Cor. 5:10).

Bob Yandian tells us that "the Greek word translated *judgment seat* is beam. The word came from the Olympic games and was the 'reward seat' on which the judge of the contest sat." The judge "would call forth the winners to appear before him to receive their rewards for their victories." Yandian goes on to say that he believes, based on the Word, that believers will only be judged for their "acts of righteousness."[1]

At the judgment seat of Christ, rewards are given out to every man according to his faithfulness. It will be Jesus Himself who will sit in the Judge's seat to hand out rewards. The Word tells us that He was exalted to this place because of His obedience in going to the cross (Phil. 2:8-11; 2 Cor. 5:10).

> For the Father judgeth no man, but hath committed all judgment unto the Son (John 5:22).

Picture what will happen. Following a royal procession, Jesus will, with all of the glory of heaven, take His seat on a throne composed of jasper, diamond and every precious gem. Then the Word tells us that every knee shall bow, and every tongue shall confess Him as Lord. Bowing at the judgment seat, we will take our crowns, millions of them, and throw them at His feet. The judgment seat of Christ is the first resurrection.

> This is the first resurrection. Blessed and holy is he that hath part in the first resurrection: on such the second death hath no power, but they shall be priests of God and of Christ, and shall reign with him a thousand years (Rev. 20:5-6).

Oral Roberts says that at the judgment seat of Christ, all believers will appear for their reward on the basis of their work done on earth. Oral says that this judgment is not to be confused with the great White Throne judgment destined for unbelievers and separated by the judgment seat of Christ by the millennium. Following the judgment in heaven, the risen redeemed, also described as the bride of Christ, shall partake of the marriage supper with Jesus Christ (Rev. 19:7-9).[2] It is following this event that Jesus will judge and hand out rewards.

Benny Hinn, in his book *The Blood*, has a unique opinion about the rewards of the believer. Hinn believes that many Christians have the wrong concept, thinking, "The Lord is going to judge us according to how we have lived, give us a mansion of gold, and that's it." Hinn believes that because of Christ's shed blood and His role as mediator, we are to receive an eternal inheritance, and he cites Hebrews 9 as support:

> And for this cause he is the mediator of the new testament, that...they which are called might receive the promise of eternal inheritance (v. 15).

Benny Hinn says: "The Bible says our inheritance is eternal, meaning it's an ongoing possession. When one reward is presented, I believe there will be another (1 Cor. 2:9; 1 Pet. 1:4)." Benny Hinn says that he is "anxious to get to glory and find out what is in store" for him.[3] I agree. This is part of the blessed hope of the church!

The Judgment of Israel

The second judgment we find in Scripture is the judgment of Israel, otherwise know as "Jacob's trouble" (Jer. 30:7). As we approach the time of the seven-year tribulation period, Israel will be confronted with whom the real

Messiah is. They will make a covenant with Antichrist for three-and-a-half years. Antichrist will turn on them and persecute the Jews, and they will face a great trial (Dan. 9:24-27).

We have a tremendous responsibility to reach out to as many Jews as possible while there is still daylight. A day is coming which will be darker than any day Israel has yet seen.

Jack Hayford in an article on prophecy, "The Church and Present Day Israel," addresses the responsibility of the church to witness to and pray for Israel now. Hayford writes, "The Bible calls us to honor the fact that since they were the national avenue by which messianic blessing has come to mankind (Rom. 9:4-5), there should be a sense of duty to 'bless' all Jewry (Gen. 12:3), to 'pray' with sincere passion for them (Rom. 10:1), and to be ready to 'bear witness' to any Jew (Rom. 1:16-17)."[4]

A Pro-Israel Charismatic Position

At this point I wish to insert a section on the pro-Israel position of charismatics. If there is any group of people who have embraced and loved the Jewish people it is the charismatic/Pentecostal camps. It is not uncommon for a charismatic church to have a Passover celebration or to use Jewish songs as a part of their regular worship. Our church, for example, has done the Passover seder several times. The last time we celebrated the Passover was with Susan Perlman, an associate executive director of Jews for Jesus. She did an incredible job of teaching our people how better to reach out to the Jewish community.

Susan works directly for Moishe Rosen, founder of Jews for Jesus, and is a part of the Lausanne Consultation on Jewish Evangelism. In a recent conversation with Perlman, she told me that Jews for Jesus has compiled statistics from their Jewish converts which indicate that charismatic/Pentecostal people have led far more Jews to Christ than any other group of Christians.

Israel Will Be Converted

Paul wrote an entire section, Romans 9–11, about the conversion of Israel in relationship to the Gentile nations. Paul was a minister to the Gentiles (Rom. 11:13), and he saw his ministry as a way to make the Jew jealous so he would convert to Jesus (Rom. 11:14). But when did Paul say that the massive conversion of Israel would take place?

> For I would not, brethren, that ye should be ignorant of this mystery...that blindness in part is happened to Israel, until the fullness of the Gentiles be come in (Rom. 11:25).

Some have compromised evangelizing the Jew by saying, "Jews have their own way of salvation through the old covenant." Others have said, "Israel is completely lost and God is finished with her; the church is spiritual Israel." Both of these extremes are wrong.

God is not finished with Israel, and it is an imperative that we reach out and evangelize the Jew as well as the Gentile in these last days. God's will is for all men to be saved (2 Pet. 3:9). "For there is no difference between the Jew and the Greek...For whosoever shall call upon the name of the Lord shall be saved" (Rom. 10:12-13).

Paul tells us that the gospel was for "the Jew first, and also to the Greek" (Rom. 1:16). We have a biblical mandate to continue evangelizing Jews as well as Gentiles.

Finis Dake, in his book of systematic theology, *God's Plan for Man*, is quick to point out that while we are to reach out to the Jew, they will not be converted in mass until the tribulation period and the return of the Lord. Dake says that the restoration of Israel will consist of Jews being gathered from every nation. "They will be gathered back unconverted (Ezek. 36:24-27). Before their conversion they will go through the greatest period of trouble they have ever gone, called the great tribulation, which will bring them back to their God. They will have a most glorious future when they are restored to favor with God and converted unto their Messiah (Zech. 12:10 – 14:21; Dan. 2:44-45; 7:13-14, 18, 27; 8:20-25; Luke 21:24; Matt. 23:38-39; 24:27-31; Rom. 11:25; Rev. 11:1-2, 15; 19:11-21)."[5] Dake is referring to the judgment of Israel.

The Witness of a Converted Jew

I had a most interesting conversation this past weekend with Paul Wilbur, a Jew who converted to Y'shua (Jesus). Paul was one of the original members of the band Harvest, and then began Israel's Hope, a Messianic band. Paul pointed out that Romans 11:12 says that Israel's conversion in the last days would be a major part of prophecy fulfilled.

> Now if the fall of them be the riches of the
> world, and the diminishing of them the riches
> of the Gentiles; how much more their fulness?
> (Rom. 11:12).

Paul Wilbur told me that he believes Israel will be prepared for mass conversion, and then Christ will return with the saints (His second coming). The fullness of Israel will mean that all nations will be blessed (Gen. 12:1-3).

Paul told me that God is calling him to take the message of the gospel through praise and worship around the world to preach to Jew and Gentile. He is preparing now to do an evangelistic taping with Integrity's Hosanna! Music live in the streets of Tel Aviv within a few months.

154

The Tabernacle of David

This brings me to worship and evangelism. We as charismatic believers have not only adopted a pro-Israel position concerning evangelism, but we also have integrated a Davidic form of worship. We owe a great debt to Israel for leading us into God's plan for praise and worship. We believe God wants to use praise and worship to evangelize the world. God Himself said:

> After this I will return, and will build again the tabernacle of David, which is fallen down; and I will build again the ruins thereof, and I will set it up: That the residue of men might seek after the Lord (Acts 15:16-17).

Jack Hayford refers to the tabernacle of David in his book *Worship His Majesty*. Hayford says this text's "focus was on 'all the nations' flowing together to the worship of God." Pastor Hayford believes that worship should be a focus of our evangelism in the last days. "It excites the imagination of those who can see that this prophecy of God's last days gathering of the nations, includes a prophecy of a last days rebuilding of a Tabernacle of David!"[6]

Hayford cites many examples (as other charismatic pastors also could) of experiences in which people are converted, healed or delivered during worship services. Worship will play a key role, not only in the conversion of gentiles, but also of Jews in the last days. Watch for worship to be a major part of end-time revival.

The Great White Throne Judgment

We have covered the judgment of believers and the judgment of Israel. Now we will cover the third judgment, the great White Throne judgment. Revelation 20 says:

But the rest of the dead lived not again until the thousand years were finished.

And I saw a great white throne, and him that sat on it, from whose face the earth and the heaven fled away; and there was found no place for them. And I saw the dead, small and great, stand before God; and the books were opened: and another book was opened, which is the book of life: and the dead were judged out of those things which were written in the books, according to their works.

And the sea gave up the dead which were in it; and death and hell delivered up the dead which were in them: and they were judged every man according to their works.

And death and hell were cast into the lake of fire. This is the second death. And whosoever was not found written in the book of life was cast into the lake of fire (Rev. 20:5,11-15).

At the end of the millennium, Satan will be cast into the lake of fire. Those who were in hell at the second coming will remain there for a thousand years until they, along with all those who did not experience salvation during the millennium, will be called to stand before God at the great White Throne judgment. Their names will not be found written in the Book of Life. This will be the judgment of all unbelievers from all of recorded history. They will have been in the holding place of hell until that time. Then hell will give up its dead, and all shall stand before a just God without excuse.

Derek Prince addresses the great White Throne judgment in his book *The Spirit-Filled Believer's Handbook*. He says this judgment "is the ultimate end of all sin and rebellion against the authority and holiness of Almighty God. Only those whose names are written in the Book of Life will escape this final judgment." Derek Prince identifies those whose names are in the book as "those who during their life on earth availed themselves, through faith, of God's mercy and grace."[7]

The Judgment of Angels

Know ye not that we shall judge angels? how much more things that pertain to this life? (1 Cor. 6:3).

This passage of Scripture has probably captured your curiosity at one time or another. Dr. Lester Sumrall, in his book *The Reality of Angels,* explains that Paul is addressing the "Corinthian Christians going to court before secular judges." These believers were suing each other. Paul tells them to work it out because one day they will judge angels. Dr. Sumrall believes this "will take place in heaven."

Dr. Sumrall asks: "Why will we judge angels? When? By what standards? What will be the results of our judgments? How is it that God sees fit to give us that responsibility?"[8]

I believe the answer to Dr. Sumrall's questions is that this text refers to our judging fallen angels. These hoards of hell have tempted the church throughout the ages. Dr. Sumrall believes the fate of these rebel angels is sealed and says that some are already in hell waiting for judgment right now. He writes, "Part of the devil's band may have been apprehended."

God spared not the angels that sinned, but cast them down to hell, and delivered them into chains of darkness, to be reserved unto judgment (2 Pet. 2:4).

Dr. Sumrall believes that a portion of these fallen angels are presently under lock and key waiting for eternal judgment, and we shall be a part of the process of judging

157

them.[9] Jude gave us further insight into this when he wrote of angels who have been reserved in everlasting chains in darkness until the great day of judgment (Jude 6).

Ultimate Judgment: The Lake of Fire

Hell was not created for mankind (Matt. 25:41); neither was the lake of fire. Hell was created as a holding place for rebellious devils until it was time to cast them into the lake of fire (Is. 14:12-20; Ezek. 28:13-19). These demonic fallen angels deserve to burn for all eternity:

> Then shall he say also unto them on the left hand, Depart from me, ye cursed, into everlasting fire, *prepared for the devil and his angels* (Matt. 25:41, italics added).

Men and women who demand to be separated from God will spend an eternity in the lake of fire. When people reject the gospel, they reject God. Without realizing it they are demanding to remain separated from Him. God only has one place where man can be separated from Him for eternity, and it is the lake of fire.

> So shall it be at the end of the world: the angels shall come forth, and sever the wicked from among the just (Matt. 13:49).

> Their the king said to the servants, Bind him hand and foot and take him away, and cast him into outer darkness; there shall be weeping and gnashing of teeth (Matt. 22:13).

> But the fearful, and unbelieving, and the abominable, and murderers, and whoremongers, and sorcerers, and idolaters, and all liars, shall have

their part in the lake which burneth with fire and brimstone: which is the second death (Rev. 21:8).

I believe that people's final rejection of the gospel before they die is what Jesus meant when He made reference to the sin of blasphemy against the Holy Spirit. All other sins, He said, could be forgiven, even sin against Him. But the Holy Spirit draws all men to salvation. The ultimate rejection of God's attempts to draw man to Himself cannot be forgiven.

The next and final chapter, "The New Heavens and The New Earth," speaks of the ultimate goal of God. Everything presses toward this revelation: it is where we shall spend all of eternity.

Practical Application

These texts and truths should motivate us to use our time and resources to win the lost to Christ so their blood will not be upon our hands.

For now you should face the future judgment with confidence and win as many souls as possible; then great will be your reward on that day. A major tool of Satan is to condemn you for your past sins. It is critical that you realize that God forgives and forgets your past sins.

You will never be able to lead others into victory if you don't have it yourself. The devil is a liar, and you have victory over him; one day you will even be a part of judging him. The next time the devil tries to remind you of your past, remind him of his future!

16

THE NEW HEAVENS AND THE NEW EARTH

The Bride of Christ

Early in my Christian walk, I was concerned about what would keep me from sinning in heaven. I did not yet have a grasp of being the righteousness of God in Christ (2 Cor. 5:21). I was still dealing with the guilt of sin. An annoying question plagued me: If Lucifer was created as the most powerful of all angels, yet he rebelled, how would I not rebel in heaven?

I asked God about this, and His Spirit spoke to my spirit in revelation knowledge. He revealed that heaven and earth would have to be recreated because Satan brought corruption intc them. He told me, "Heaven will have to be recreated because of the marring and the memory of Satan's rebellion there. Earth will have to be recreated because Satan brought sin here." In order for God to remove all memory of sin and rebellion, He will recreate both the heavens and earth.

In the new heavens and the new earth there shall be no memory of sin, the past or unsaved loved ones who did not make it. All that Satan has done and influenced will be removed. Revelation 21:4 tells us:

> And God shall wipe away all tears from their eyes;
> and there shall be no more death, neither sorrow,
> nor crying, neither shall there be any more pain:
> for the former things are passed away.

The "former things" are those things with which we wrestle in the here and now — death, sorrow and pain. Even in the midst of knowing that we have victory in Christ, we must wrestle against principalities, powers and forces of darkness.

We charismatics generally believe that we experience the "firstfruits of the Spirit" (Rom. 8:23), the foretaste of the kingdom, right now. But we also realize that God has set an appointed time in the future when the kingdom will be fully consummated, or brought into fullness. The establishment of the kingdom in fullness will be greater than any of us can imagine.

That which makes life painful and difficult for us now will be swept away on the day of the Lord's final judgment. "The heavens will disappear with a roar; the elements will be destroyed by fire, and the earth and everything in it will be laid bare" (2 Pet. 3:10, NIV). Those things which caused sorrow will flee away together with the earth and the heavens (Rev. 20:11).

Isaiah predicted much the same thing over seven hundred years earlier:

> Lift up your eyes to the heavens, and look upon the earth beneath: for the heavens shall vanish away like smoke, and the earth shall wax old like a garment (Is. 51:6).

> For, behold, I create new heavens and a new earth; and the former shall not be remembered, nor come into mind (Is. 65:17).

By creating the new heavens and the new earth, God instantly removes all of the former things which brought sorrow to our lives. There will be no more death because there will be no more sin. And the one who held the power of death, the devil, will have been destroyed. Both death and the devil will be thrown into the lake of fire (Rev. 20:10,14) just prior to the arrival of the new heavens, the new earth and the holy city, the new Jerusalem.

The New Jerusalem

God will create a "new heaven and a new earth: for the first heaven and the first earth were passed away; and there was no more sea" (Rev. 21:1). Then John writes that he "saw the holy city, new Jerusalem, coming down from God" (21:2).

Rod Parsley, in *Holiness: Living Leaven Free*, says that God will bring "the new city, the new Jerusalem, the city of the great King. God will wipe away the tears." He continues, "A new Jerusalem is coming, where the glory of God will shine upon all who get the leaven out."[1]

In his commentary on the New Testament, Oral Roberts says, "The city of God is 1500 miles in height and length on each side. It is a perfect square. And it is adorned with all types of precious stones." The new Jerusalem shall be adorned with precious products that are not conceivable to our imaginations because they have not been created yet —

gold that will be transparent like glass and pearls three-hundred-feet thick. The sun will not be needed because God shall be the light there. What a tremendous place!

Oral Roberts is quick to say that more important than the beauty of the city is the fact that "the Lord God and the Lamb are the temple of the city of God. Just as God walked and talked with Adam and Eve in the garden of Eden, so He will be restored to His rightful place as the temple of his people" (Rev. 21:9-27). Oral says, "The Heaven of all heavens is the Lord."[2]

The new Jerusalem is described in the same language which John used earlier to describe the church: The "wife hath made herself ready" (Rev. 19:7); the church is "prepared as a bride adorned for her husband" (Rev. 21:2). The new Jerusalem is clearly the church, the bride of Christ.

Then, according to John, "The tabernacle of God is with men, and he will dwell with them, and they shall be his people, and God himself shall be with them, and be their God" (Rev. 21:3). God will personally wipe the tears from every eye. The Lord God Almighty and the Lamb, Jesus Christ our Lord, will be the temple in new Jerusalem, the holy city that is the church glorified, the church triumphant (Rev. 21:22).

This is the ultimate purpose of the church. This is where we are all headed. Is it any wonder that John closes the book of Revelation with, "Even so, come, Lord Jesus" (22:20). Yes! Amen.

Practical Application

In closing I would like to give you ten things you can put into practice as a result of having studied about the end times. I believe God is speaking these truths to the church in these final hours.

1. Live every day as if Jesus could return at any moment, yet plan to occupy until He comes. God placed a divine tension in the Scriptures that His Son can come at any moment. The doctrine of imminence should motivate us to live holy lives, to live on the edge.

2. Preach and teach on the second coming of Christ regularly. We need more preaching, not only on the second coming, but also on heaven and hell. These doctrines also have the unique ability to comfort and motivate the believer to work for the expansion of the kingdom (1 Thess. 4:18; 1 Cor. 15:58).

3. Let the knowledge that Jesus is coming soon motivate you to win souls. I believe the doctrine of end times to be one of the most evangelistic doctrines of the church. When a person shares or preaches on the end times, the conversation naturally comes around to where you will spend eternity!

4. Be found praying and obeying when Jesus returns. I want to be found on the cutting edge, praying for an end-time anointing and operating in His will for my life.

5. Use the Word to interpret the events in society as signs, and share them with your generation. You have a responsibility to know what is going on around you in the world. God has designed the Word to be lived out prophetically in every society. Know the Word and interpret it to your world.

6. Be in a church that has the five-fold ministry operating in it; then you will be part of the bride

without spot or wrinkle. A pastor who is strong in the Word often invites guest speakers who operate as apostles, prophets, evangelists and teachers. These gifts are necessary to equip the end-time church to do the work of the ministry (Eph. 4:11-12).

7. Keep looking up, no matter how bad things get around you. Remember that your redemption draweth nigh! The blessed hope of Jesus' return is to be a sure foundation during the hard times of trial and temptation. Stand fast during your most difficult situations, knowing that you win in the end.

8. Find your purpose and vocation in life; fulfill the will of God with excellence, and you will have great rewards. You will be rewarded now, in the millennium and at the judgment seat of the believer. What you do now will most definitely affect your future.

9. Know that God, not the devil, is in control of the end times, and His timetable is right on schedule. Again, no matter how bad things in society appear to be getting, never think that the devil is in control. He knows his time is short, but he can only do what God and the church allow him to do. Certain future events are written, and they will come to pass.

10. Make real long-term goals in light of the millennium and the new heavens and earth. The time span of our life is short compared to a thou-sand years, let alone eternity.

I would like to share a final word of blessing for those of you who have read this book. There is a promise to you who study prophecy with the purpose of obeying the Word: "Blessed is he that readeth, and they that hear the words of this prophecy, and keep those things which are written therein: for the time is at hand" (Rev. 1:3).

Charismatic theology is practical and exciting. As you fulfill the words of Christ in these last days you will have an increased anointing; you will do great exploits. Accomplish what God has for your life, remembering that ultimately we will all live together forever in a place greater than the garden of Eden. The new Jerusalem is a far more spectacular place than anything ever created. Get ready because He's coming soon!

MARANATHA!

FLOW CHART OF END-TIME BIBLICAL EVENTS

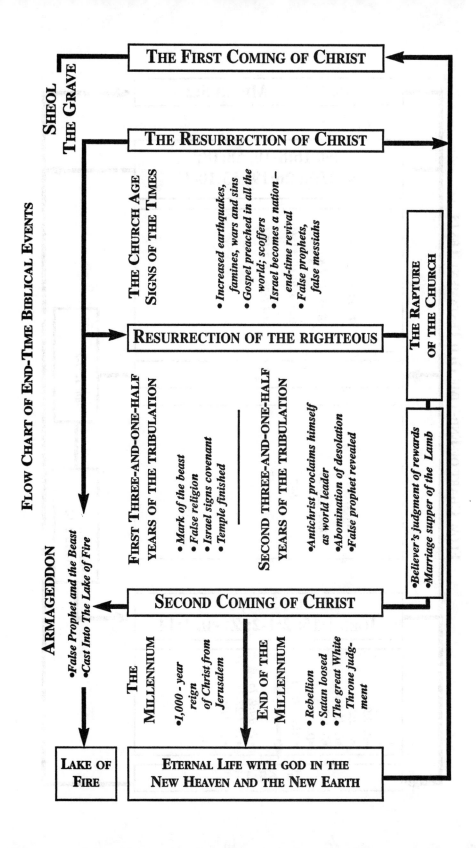

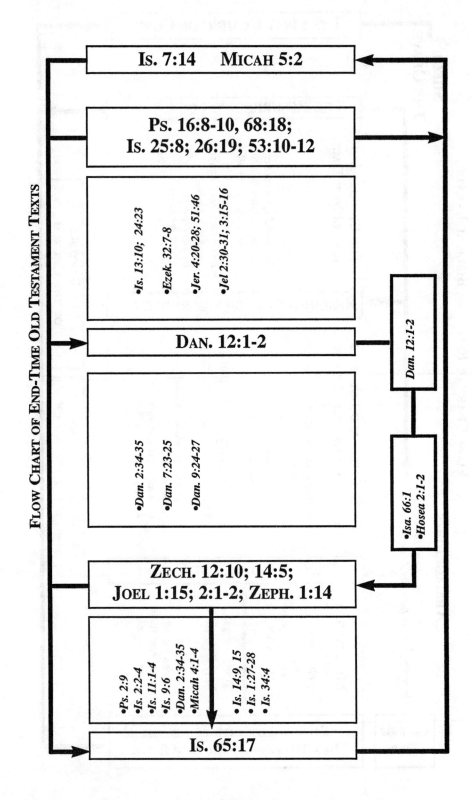

FLOW CHART OF END-TIME OLD TESTAMENT TEXTS

IS. 7:14   MICAH 5:2

PS. 16:8-10, 68:18;
IS. 25:8; 26:19; 53:10-12

•Is. 13:10; 24:23
•Ezek. 32:7-8
•Jer. 4:20-28; 51:46
•Jel 2:30-31; 3:15-16

DAN. 12:1-2

Dan. 12:1-2

•Dan. 2:34-35
•Dan. 7:23-25
•Dan. 9:24-27

•Isa. 66:1
•Hosea 2:1-2

ZECH. 12:10; 14:5;
JOEL 1:15; 2:1-2; ZEPH. 1:14

•Ps. 2:9
•Is. 2:2-4
•Is. 11:1-4
•Is. 9:6
•Dan. 2:34-35
•Micah 4:1-4

• Is. 14:9, 15
• Is. 1:27-28
• Is. 34:4

IS. 65:17

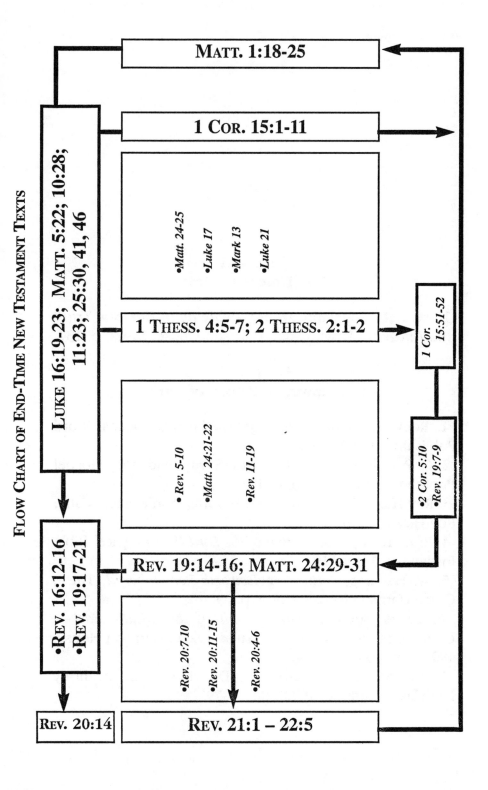

FLOW CHART OF END-TIME NEW TESTAMENT TEXTS

MATT. 1:18-25

1 COR. 15:1-11

•Matt. 24-25
•Luke 17
•Mark 13
•Luke 21

LUKE 16:19-23; MATT. 5:22; 10:28;
11:23; 25:30, 41, 46

1 THESS. 4:5-7; 2 THESS. 2:1-2

1 Cor. 15:51-52

•Rev. 5-10
•Matt. 24:21-22
•Rev. 11-19

•2 Cor. 5:10
•Rev. 19:7-9

•REV. 16:12-16
•REV. 19:17-21

REV. 19:14-16; MATT. 24:29-31

•Rev. 20:7-10
•Rev. 20:11-15
•Rev. 20:4-6

REV. 20:14

REV. 21:1 – 22:5

Notes

Chapter 1
The Time Is Critical

1. Kenneth Copeland, *Honor–Walking in Honesty, Truth and Integrity* (Tulsa, Okla.: Harrison House, 1992), p. 137.

Chapter 2
The Imminent Return of Christ

1. Reinhard Bonnke, *Evangelism by Fire* (Dallas: Word Publishing, 1990), pp. 20-21.
2. C. P. Nelson, *Bible Doctrines* (Springfield, Mo.: Gospel Publishing House, 1948), p. 127.
3. Roy Hicks, *Final Days and Counting* (San Marcos, Calif.: Roy Hicks, 1990), p. 9.
4. R. A. Torrey, *The Return of the Lord* (Los Angeles: Bible Institute, 1913), p. 19.
5. W. Hacking, *Smith Wigglesworth Remembered* (Tulsa, Okla.: Harrison House, 1981), p. 69.
6. Lester Sumrall, *Time Bomb in the Middle East — Countdown to Armageddon* (Tulsa, Okla.: Harrison House, 1991), pp. 106, 111.
7. Mario Murillo, *Fresh Fire* (Danville, Calif.: Anthony Douglas Publishing, 1991), pp. 77-79.

Chapter 3
End-Time Harvest

1. Gordon Lindsay, *The World: 2000 A.D.* (Dallas: Christ for the Nations, 1968), pp. 90-92.

2. Rex Humbard, *The Third Dimension* (Old Tappan, N.J.: Fleming Revell Co., 1972), p. 137.

3. Lester Sumrall, *I Predict 2000 A.D.* (South Bend, Ind.: LESA Publishing Co., 1987), pp. 74-76.

4. Michael Wourms, *The Chosen Warrior* (Lake Mary, Fla.: Creation House, 1989), pp. 216-217. This book is about the ministry of Morris Cerullo.

5. Morris Cerullo, *Victory Miracle Library,* May 1990, p. 2. This magazine is published by Morris Cerullo World Evangelism in San Diego, California.

6. David Shibley, *A Force in the Earth* (Lake Mary, Fla.: Creation House, 1990), pp. 26-29.

7. William DeArteaga, *Quenching the Spirit* (Lake Mary, Fla.: Creation House, 1992), pp. 14-15.

8. Murillo, *Fresh Fire,* pp. 77-79.

9. Maria Woodworth-Etter, *A Diary of Signs and Wonders* (Tulsa, Okla.: Harrison House; original copyright by M.B.W. Etter, 1916), pp. 187-190.

10. This and other Kuhlman material can be found at the archives in the Wheaton College Library, Wheaton, Illinois.

11. Daisy Washburn Osborn, *Five Choices for Women Who Win* (Tulsa, Okla.: OSFO Books, 1986), pp. 44-45.

12. Frederick Price, *Practical Suggestions for Successful Ministry* (Tulsa, Okla.: Harrison House, 1991), p. 70.

13. Paul Crouch, *I Had No Father But God* (Santa Ana, Calif.: Trinity Broadcasting Network, 1993), p. 138.

14. Ibid., p. 142.

15. Ibid., p. 230.

16. CBN Public Relations Division, Virginia Beach, Virginia, 1995.

17. From the missions statement of The Christian Broadcasting Network, Inc. (Virginia Beach, Va.: Public Relations Division, 1995).
18. CBN Public Relations Division, Virginia Beach, Virginia, 1995.
19. Torrey, *The Return of the Lord*, p. 20.

Chapter 4
Which Generation Will Be the Last?

1. Carman Licciardello, *Raising the Standard* (Nashville, Tenn.: Sparrow Press, 1994), p. 185.
2. Roberts Liardon, *Final Approach* (Lake Mary, Fla.: Creation House, 1993), pp. 17-18.
3. Pat Robertson, *The New World Order* (Dallas, Tex.: Word Publishing, 1991), pp. 48-49, 119-120, 145, 226.
   Hal Lindsey, *The Collected Works of Hal Lindsey* (New York: Inspiration Press, 1991), pp. 119-120.
4. Sumrall, *Time Bomb*, pp. 105-106.
5. Licciardello, *Raising the Standard*, p. 189.
6. Ibid., p. 188.
7. Benny Hinn, *The Anointing* (Nashville, Tenn.: Thomas Nelson, 1992), pp. 143-150.

Chapter 5
Signs of the Times

1. Charles Capps, from the message "Signposts Along the Way" given at Calvary Lighthouse Church, Rochelle, Ill., 29 May 1993, at which the author was present.
2. John Ankerberg, ed., *One World: Biblical Prophecy and the New World Order* (Chicago, Ill.: Moody Press, 1991), pp. 55-56.
3. Oral Roberts, *God's Timetable for the End Time!* (Tulsa, Okla.: Heliotrope Publications, 1969), p. 61.
4. Liardon, *Final Approach*, p. 27.

5. Richard Eby, *Didn't You Read My Book?* (Shippensburg, Pa.: Companion Press, 1991), *p. 135.*

6. *Mike Evans,* The Return (Nashville, Tenn.: Thomas Nelson, 1986), p. 207.

7. Finis Jennings Dake, *The Second Coming of Christ* (Atlanta, Ga.: Bible Research Foundation, 1955), pp. 29-31.

8. Marilyn Hickey, *Signs in the Heavens* (Denver: Marilyn Hickey Ministries, 1984), pp. 10-11.

9. Aimee Semple McPherson, *The Second Coming of Christ* (Los Angeles: Aimee Semple McPherson Evangelistic Assoc., 1921), pp. 47-48.

10. Oral Roberts, *The Drama of the End Time* (Tulsa, Okla.: Oral Roberts Evangelistic Assoc., 1969), pp. 17-18.

11. C. M. Ward, *...Waiting...* (Springfield, Mo.: Gospel Publishing House, 1959), pp. 17-26.

12. Sumrall, *I Predict 2000 A.D.,* p. 109.

13. Woodworth-Etter, *A Diary of Signs and Wonders,* p. 227.

14. Roberts, *The Drama of the End Time,* p. 11.

Chapter 6
Prepare!

1. Jamie Buckingham, *Parables* (Lake Mary, Fla.: Creation House, 1991), pp. 61-74.

2. Rodney M. Howard-Browne, *The Touch of God* (Louisville, Ky.: R.H.B.E.A. Publications, 1992), pp. 87,90.

3. Gloria Copeland, *Build Yourself an Ark* (Fort Worth, Tex.: Kenneth Copeland Publications, 1992), pp. 58-59.

4. Ibid., p. 59.

5. David Yonggi Cho, *Prayer: Key to Revival* (Waco, Tex.: Word Book Publishers, 1984), pp. 157-158. Dr. Cho changed his name from "Paul Yonggi" to "David Yonggi." The latter will be used through the remainder of this book.

6. David Wilkerson, *Racing Toward Judgment* (Lindale, Tex.: Youth Crusades, 1976), pp. 114-115.

7. Francis Frangipane, *Holiness, Truth, and the Presence of God* (Cedar Rapids, Iowa: Arrow Publications, 1986), pp. 67-68.

8. John Avanzini, *God's Law of Retribution* (San Diego: Morris Cerullo World Evangelism, 1984), pp. 90-91.

9. Rod Parsley, *Tribulation to Triumph* (Tulsa, Okla.: Harrison House, 1991), pp. 17-18.

10. Lori Wilke, *The Costly Anointing* (Shippensburg: Destiny Image, 1991), p. 111.

11. Kim Clement, *The Sound of His Voice* (Lake Mary, Fla.: Creation House, 1993), p. 152.

12. Howard-Browne, *The Touch of God*, p. 89.

13. Ibid., p. 92.

Chapter 7
The Premillennial Return of Christ

1. David Yonggi Cho, *Revelation* (Lake Mary, Fla.: Creation House, 1991), p. 54.

2. Marilyn Hickey, *Armageddon* (Denver: Marilyn Hickey Ministries, 1994), p. 6.

3. Hilton Sutton, *Rapture: Get Right or Get Left* (Tulsa, Okla.: Harrison House, 1983), p. 51.

4. Hal Lindsey, *The Road to Holocaust* (New York: Bantam Books, 1989), p. 27.

5. Ibid., p. 194

6. Thomas Reid et al., *Seduction? A Biblical Response* (New Wilmington, Pa.: Son-Rise Publications, 1986), pp. 160,164.

7. H. Wayne House and Thomas Ice, *Dominion Theology: Blessing or Curse?* (Portland, Ore.: Multnomah Press, 1988), pp. 15-16.

8. Ibid., p. 16.

9. Lindsey, *The Road to Holocaust*, p. 30.

10. Dake, *The Second Coming of Christ*, pp. 24-25.

11. Nelson, *Bible Doctrines*, p. 136.

12. John F. Walvoord, *The Prophecy Knowledge Handbook* (Wheaton, Ill.: Victor Books, 1990), p. 16.
13. Ibid.

Chapter 8
The Rapture of the Church

1. Sutton, *Rapture*, p. 47.
2. Ibid., p. 7.
3. Roberts, *God's Timetable*, p. 61.
4. Jack Van Impe, *11:59...and Counting* (Troy, Mich.: Jack Van Impe Ministries, 1983), p. 12.
5. Bob Yandian, *Resurrection — Our Victory Over Death* (Tulsa, Okla.: Harrison House, 1986), p. 88.
6. Roy Hicks, *Another Look at the Rapture*, (Tulsa, Okla.: Harrison House, 1982), p. 39.
7. Hickey, *Armageddon*, p. 20.
8. Ibid., p. 21.
9. T. J. McCrossan, *Bodily Healing and the Atonement*, ed. by Roy Hicks and Kenneth Hagin (Tulsa, Okla.: Faith Library, 1982), pp. 69-71.
10 Billy Graham, *World Aflame* (Minneapolis, Minn.: Billy Graham Evangelistic Association, 1965), p. 189.
11. Oral Roberts, *The New Testament Comes Alive*, vol. 1, (Nashville, Tenn.: Parthenon Press, 1984), p. 130.
12. Ibid., p. 132.
13. McPherson, *The Second Coming of Christ*, pp. 32-33.
14. Dake, *The Second Coming of Christ*, p. 21.
15. Yandian, *Resurrection*, pp. 96,101.
16. Frederick Price, *Concerning Them Which Are Asleep* (Tulsa, Okla.: Harrison House, 1989), p. 11.
17. Yandian, *Resurrection*, pp. 96,101.
18. Hicks, *Another Look at the Rapture*, p. 45.
19. Licciardello, *Raising the Standard*, pp. 187-188.
20. Ibid., p. 195.
21. Ibid.

22. Roberts, *God's Timetable,* p. 65.
23. Ibid.
24. Ibid.
25. Roberts Liardon, *Run to the Battle* (Tulsa, Okla.: Harrison House, 1989), p. 23.

Chapter 9
Pretribulation

1. Hickey, *Armageddon,* pp. 19,23.
2. Hicks, Another Look at the Rapture (Tulsa, Okla.: Harrison House, 1982), p. 39.
3. Roberts, *The New Testament Comes Alive,* vol. 1, p. 130.

Chapter 10
Daniel: One Week Until Midnight

1. David Yonggi Cho, *Daniel* (Lake Mary, Fla.: Creation House, 1991), pp. 117-119.
2. Carlton Pearson, *I've Got a Feelin' Everything's Gonna Be All Right!* (Tulsa, Okla.: Harrison House, 1992), pp. 204-205.
3. Ibid.
4. Clement, *The Sound of His Voice,* p. 172.
5. Roberts, *God's Timetable,* p. 77.
6. Walvoord, *The Prophecy Knowledge Handbook,* pp. 248-256.
7. Hickey, *Armageddon,* p. 24.
8. Sumrall, *Time Bomb,* p. 34.
9. Lindsey, *The Collected Works of Hal Lindsey,* p. 42.
10. Roberts, *The New Testament Comes Alive,* vol. 1, p. 129.

Chapter 11
John's Revelation of Christ

1. Cho, *Revelation,* p. 9.
2. Marilyn Hickey, *The Book of Revelation* (Denver: Marilyn Hickey Ministries, 1987), pp. 17-18.

3. Cho, *Revelation,* p. 103.
4. Marilyn Hickey, *The Book of Revelation,* p. 109.
5. Hickey, Armageddon, p. 38
6. Joseph Good, *Rosh Hashanah and the Messianic Kingdom to Come* (Port Arthur, Tex.: Hatika Ministries, 1989), p. 36.
7. Walvoord, *The Prophecy Knowledge Handbook,* p. 387.

Chapter 12
The Millennium – Now or Later?

1. See George E. Ladd, *A Theology of the New Testament* (Grand Rapids, Mich.: Eerdmans Publishing, 1974), for more information on this subject.
2. Larry Lea, *The Weapons of Your Warfare* (Lake Mary, Fla.: Creation House, 1989), p. 20.
3. Jack W. Hayford, "A Present and Future Kingdom," *The Spirit Filled Life Bible,* New King James Version, edited by Jack Hayford, Litt.D. (Nashville, Tenn.: Thomas Nelson, 1991), p. 1,428.
4. Tommy Reid, *Kingdom Now But Not Yet,* (Buffalo, N.Y.: 1 JN Publishing, 1988), p. xvii.
5. Pat Robertson and Bob Slosser, *The Secret Kingdom* (Nashville, Tenn.: Thomas Nelson, 1982), pp. 216-217.
6. Bob Yandian, *Salt and Light* (Tulsa, Okla.: Harrison House, 1983), pp. 86-88.
7. Robertson, *The Secret Kingdom,* p. 218.
8. Bob Yandian, *One Nation Under God* (Tulsa, Okla.: Harrison House, 1988), pp. 50-51.
9. Robertson, *The Secret Kingdom,* p. 211.
10. Robertson, *The New World Order,* pp. 247-248,268.

Chapter 13
The Millennial Reign of Christ

1. Sumrall, *Time Bomb,* pp. 93-94.
2. William Menzies and Stanley Horton, *Bible Doctrines: A*

Pentecostal Perspective (Springfield, Mo.: Logion Press, 1993), p. 231.

3. Sumrall, *Time Bomb*, pp. 96-97.

4. Robertson, *The Secret Kingdom*, p. 219.

5. Robertson, *The New World Order*, p. 250.

6. Gordon Lindsay, *A Thousand Years of Peace* (Dallas: Christ for the Nations Publication, 1974), p. 5.

7. Ibid., p. 21.

8. Roberts, *The New Testament Comes Alive*, vol. 3, p. 153.

Chapter 14
A Literal Heaven and Hell

1. Rod Parsley, *Holiness: Living Leaven Free* (Columbus, Ohio: Results Publishing, 1993), p. 96.

2. Creflo A. Dollar Jr., *Heaven and Hell* (College Park, Ga.: World Changers Ministries, 1993), p. 1.

3. Parsley, *Holiness*, p. 94.

4. Myles Munroe, *Understanding Your Potential* (Shippensburg, Pa.: Destiny Image Publishers, 1991), pp. 81-83.

5. Kenneth E. Hagin, *Zoe: The God Kind of Life* (Tulsa, Okla.: Faith Library Publications, 1993), pp. 9,27,47,48.

6. Joyce Meyer, *Beauty for Ashes* (Tulsa, Okla.: Harrison House, 1994), pp. 155-156.

7. T. D. Jakes, *Can You Stand to Be Blessed?* (Shippensburg, Pa.: Destiny Image, 1994), p. 69.

8. Benny Hinn, *War in the Heavenlies* (Dallas: Heritage Publishers, 1984), pp. 63-71.

9. Dollar, *Heaven and Hell*, pp. 6-7.

10. Hinn, *War in the Heavenlies*, pp. 63-71.

11. Wourms, *The Chosen Warrior*, p. 91-101.

12. Dwight Thompson, *Devil, You Can't Have My Family* (Tulsa, Okla.: Harrison House, 1993), p. 23.

13. Ibid., p. 29.

14. Roberts, *God's Timetable*, pp. 93-96.

15. Woodworth-Etter, *A Diary of Signs and Wonders*, p. 187.

16. Dollar, *Heaven and Hell,* p. 5.
17. Maria Woodworth-Etter, *A Diary of Signs and Wonders,* pp. 188-190.
18. Ibid., p. 190.
19. Richard Roberts, *How You Can Touch Heaven With Your Faith* (Tulsa, Okla.: Richard Roberts, 1991), p. 94.

Chapter 15
The Final Judgment

1. Yandian, *Resurrection,* pp. 91-92.
2. Roberts, *God's Timetable,* p. 62.
3. Benny Hinn, *The Blood* (Lake Mary, Fla.: Creation House, 1993), pp. 118-119.
4. Hayford, "The Church and Present Day Israel," *The Spirit Filled Life Bible,* p. 1,706.
5. Finis Jennings Dake, *God's Plan for Man* (Lawrenceville, Ga.: Dake Bible Sales, 1949), p. 319.
6. Jack W. Hayford, *Worship His Majesty* (Waco, Tex.: Word Books, 1987), pp. 136-137.
7. Derek Prince, *The Spirit-filled Believer's Handbook* (Lake Mary, Fla.: Creation House, 1993), p. 513.
8. Sumrall, *The Reality of Angels,* p. 126.
9. Ibid., p. 109.

Chapter 16
The New Heavens and the New Earth

1. Parsley, *Holiness,* pp. 94-96.
2. Roberts, *The New Testament Comes Alive,* vol. 3, pp. 154-155.

Glossary

AMILLENNIAL: This term literally means "no millennium." Amillennialism was proposed by Augustine in the latter part of the fourth century. It suggests the millennium to be the thousand years beginning at the cross and ending theoretically at the second coming of Christ.

ABOMINATION OF DESOLATION: An event which will take place midway through the tribulation period in which the Anti-christ will set himself up in the temple in Jerusalem to be worshipped as a god.

ANTICHRIST: This expression means "that which is against Christ," and refers to a person whom Satan will anoint as a world leader in the last days.

ARMAGEDDON: The place of the final battle where the Anti-christ's armies and the kings of the West meet the kings of the East. The term comes from the Hebrew expression *har,* which means "hill or mountain," in this case of Megiddo.

CONSUMMATION: The completion of things. This is a reference to the kingdom of God coming in fullness or completion.

DISPENSATIONS: Periods of time in which God has administered His grace to mankind according to His plan for that time period, which may be different from His plan for another time period. These are not to be confused with the system of theology called dispensationalism.

DOCTRINE: This term actually means "to teach." The teaching, or dogma, of Scripture makes up Christian doctrine, which is that which Christians believe.

ESCHATOLOGY: The doctrine of the end times, or last things. From the Greek *eschatos,* meaning "end," and *ology,* meaning "science, or study of."

FINAL JUDGMENT: The event at which God will judge mankind for sin.

GEHENNA: A place of eternal punishment cited by Christ in Matthew 25:46; 5:22; 23:33; Mark 9:47-48; Rev. 14:11; 20:14.

GREAT TRIBULATION: This expression is from the two Greek words, *mega,* meaning "great," and *thlipsis,* meaning "pressure, anguish, trials or persecution." This refers to the seven-year period when God pours out His wrath upon the earth.

IMMINENCE: The doctrine which maintains that Christ's return could occur at any time, and is imminent.

HELL: A temporary holding place for the unsaved which itself shall ultimately be cast into the lake of fire. It is also known as *Sheol* (the Hebrew equivalent of the Greek word *Hades*).

KINGDOM-NOW: A system of belief based on postmillennial thinking, also known as reconstructionism or dominionism. It maintains that the kingdom of God has arrived, and we are living in it now.

LAKE OF FIRE: The eternal place of torment for the devil and his angels, as well as for anyone who does not receive God's gift of grace, Jesus. It is the place of eternal separation from God.

MARK OF THE BEAST: A mark which the Antichrist, otherwise known as the beast, will require all people on the earth to take on the right hand or on the forehead.

MIDTRIBULATIONIST: A person who believes that Jesus will rapture the church midway through the tribulation period.

MILLENNIUM: A period of a thousand years. This refers to the literal period of time which begins after the seven-year tribulation has ended and ends before the creation of the new heavens and the new earth.

NEW HEAVENS AND NEW EARTH: The eternal place of restoration where God dwells with man and removes the former things. Here there will be no memory of sorrow or pain, only eternal peace.

PAROUSIA: A Greek word meaning "to be with" or "the advent or return." Here this refers to the return of Christ for His church.

PRAGMATIC THEOLOGY: Theology that is practiced on a day-to-day basis, is practical and can be worked out in everyday life.

PRETRIBULATIONIST: A person who believes that Jesus will rapture the church at the beginning of the tribulation period.

POSTMILLENNIAL: This term literally means "after or at the end of the millennium," and refers to the belief that the second coming of Christ will be at the end of the millennium. This concept was developed by the church fathers of the second century, and has many variations to it.

POSTTRIBULATIONIST: A person who believes that Jesus will rapture the church at the end of the tribulation period.

PREMILLENNIAL: The term literally means "before the millennium." Premillennialists expect the second coming of Jesus before the millennium.

PROPHECY: From the Old Testament expression in the Hebrew, *nabiy*, meaning "mouth piece." Prophecy does two things: it foretells, and it forth tells. Foretelling speaks of the future. Forth telling is speaking forth exhortation, encouragement and comfort for the present.

RAPTURE: From the Latin word *rapio,* meaning "the snatching or catching away." This refers to the saints being caught up in the air to be united with Jesus, and should not be confused with the second coming.

SECOND COMING OF CHRIST: The time when Jesus will return with His saints to make war with the Antichrist and his armies and set up His reign on earth.

SYSTEMATIC THEOLOGY: A system by which the major doctrines of the church are developed by compiling proofs from both Old and New Testaments in a systematic way.

THEOLOGY: The science or study of the things of God. It comes from the two Greek words, *theo,* meaning "god," and *ology,* meaning "study of."

TRIBULATION PERIOD: A specific period of time of great trouble or pressure when God pours out his wrath upon the earth. This expression in the Greek, *thlipsis,* means "pressure, anguish, trials or persecution.

Scripture Index

Name Index

If you enjoyed *He's Coming Soon*, we would like
to recommend the following books:

Final Approach
by Roberts Liardon

Sometimes Christians get so caught up in debates about
the end times that they forget the real purpose for being
here on earth. That's the foundational truth behind Roberts
Liardon's latest release, *Final Approach*. It offers readers a
refreshing, positive guide to living in the end times.

Revelation
by David Yonggi Cho

David Yonggi Cho is pastor of the world's largest
church, the Full Gospel Church in Seoul, Korea. In his book
Revelation he unlocks the mystery behind the symbolism
of this difficult yet fascinating book of the Bible. He relates
past and present world events to the words recorded by
the apostle John.

The Next Move of God
by Fuchsia Pickett

As the charismatic movement continues to grow, many
wonder where it's headed. What is the next move of God?
Author Fuchsia Pickett illustrates the coming new wave of
the Holy Spirit. This message will be of particular interest to
those who have been involved in the prophetic interpretation of Scripture.

Available at your local Christian bookstore or from:

Creation House
600 Rinehart Road
Lake Mary, FL 32746
1-800-283-8494